MACHINE LEARNING AND BIOMETRICS

Edited by **Jucheng Yang, Dong Sun Park, Sook Yoon, Yarui Chen** and **Chuanlei Zhang**

Machine Learning and Biometrics

http://dx.doi.org/10.5772/intechopen.71297
Edited by Jucheng Yang, Dong Sun Park, Sook Yoon, Yarui Chen and Chuanlei Zhang

Contributors

Evon M.O. Abu-Taieh, Hamed S. Al-Bdour, Ryszard S. Choras, Serestina Viriri, Abdelgader Abdelwhab, Shaojie Chen, Qing Zhao, Martin Drahansky, Jucheng Yang, Lingchao Zhang, Meng Li, Tingting Zhao, Yarui Chen, Jianzheng Liu, Na Liu

Notice

First published in London, United Kingdom, 2018 by IntechOpen
IntechOpen is the global imprint of INTECHOPEN LIMITED, registered in England and Wales, registration number: 11086078, The Shard, 25th floor, 32 London Bridge Street
London, SE19SG – United Kingdom
Printed in Croatia

British Library Cataloguing-in-Publication Data
A catalogue record for this book is available from the British Library

Additional hard copies can be obtained from orders@intechopen.com

Machine Learning and Biometrics, Edited by Jucheng Yang, Dong Sun Park, Sook Yoon, Yarui Chen and Chuanlei Zhang
p. cm.
Print ISBN 978-1-78923-590-6
Online ISBN 978-1-78923-591-3

For EU product safety concerns:
IN TECH d.o.o., Prolaz Marije Krucifikse Kozulić 3, 51000 Rijeka, Croatia,
info@intechopen.com or visit our website at intechopen.com.

Meet the editors

Jucheng Yang is a special professor at the College of Computer Science and Information Engineering, Tianjin University of Science and Technology, Tianjin, China. He received his BS degree from the South Central University for Nationalities, China, and his MS and PhD degrees from the Chonbuk National University, Republic of Korea. He was a visiting professor at the University of New South Wales, Australia and University of Surrey, UK. He has published over 100 papers in related to international journals and conferences. He served as an editor or a reviewer of international journals, such as *IEEE Transactions on Information Forensics & Security, IEEE Transactions on Industrial Informatics, IEEE Communications Magazine,* and *IEEE Transactions on Circuits and Systems for Video Technology, Science China,* the chairman of 6 conferences, and a PC member of over 20 conferences. He has applied 50 Chinese patents and was awarded 10 Chinese patents of biometrics. His research interests include biometrics, image processing, pattern recognition, and neural networks.

Yarui Chen is an associate professor at the College of Computer Science and Information Engineering, Tianjin University of Science and Technology, Tianjin, P.R. China. She received her BS degree from the Hebei University of Technology, China, and her MS and PhD degrees from the Tianjin University, China. She has published nearly 20 papers in related to international journals and conferences. She served as a reviewer of international journals, such as *Neurocomputing, Artificial Intelligence Review,* and *KSII Transactions on Internet and Information Systems*. Her research interests include machine learning, neural networks, probabilistic inference, and approximate inference.

Chuanlei Zhang is an associate professor at the College of Computer Science and Information Engineering, Tianjin University of Science and Technology, Tianjin, P.R. China. He was born on October 09, 1973, and received his BS degree from the Taiyuan University of Technology and his MS and PhD degrees from the China University of Mining and Technology (Beijing), China, in 1995, 1998, and 2006, respectively, all in Electrical Engineering. Since September 2010, he has been working at the Department of Electrical and Computer Engineering, Ryerson University, Toronto, Canada, where he was a postdoctorate student of the Communication and Signal Processing Applications Laboratory (CASPAL). Prior to joining Ryerson, from 2000 to

2010, he was a software manager and a senior software engineer at Motorola (China). From 1998 to 2010, he was a senior software engineer at the Beijing Research Institute of Water Affairs and Automation, China. He is a reviewer of several journals and international conferences, including the *Journal of CUMT Mining Science and Technology*. He is a member of IEEE and a senior member of the Chinese Institute of Electronics. His research interests include pattern recognition and artificial neural network, data mining, signal processing, wireless communication, multimedia retrieval and video content analysis, computational intelligence, and applications in bioinformatics and finance.

Dong Sun Park is a professor at the Division of Electronics Engineering, Chonbuk National University, South Korea. He received his BS degree from the Department of Electronics Engineering, Korea University, South Korea, in 1979, and his MS and PhD degrees from the University of Missouri, USA, in 1984 and 1990, respectively. His research interests include deep neural networks, biometrics, and computer vision.

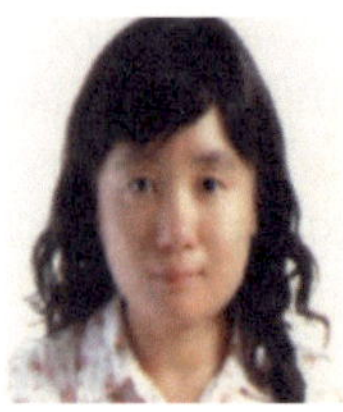

Sook Yoon is a professor at the Mokpo National University, South Korea. She received her PhD degree in Electronics Engineering from the Chonbuk National University, Korea, in 2003. She was a researcher in Electrical Engineering and Computer Sciences at the University of California, Berkeley, USA, until June 2006. She joined the Mokpo National University in September 2006. Currently, she is a professor at the Department of Computer Engineering, Mokpo National University. She was a visiting scholar at the Utah Center of Advanced Imaging Research, University of Utah, USA, from 2013 to 2015. Her main research interests include image processing and computer vision, object recognition, machine learning, and biometrics.

Contents

Preface

In recent years, biometric researches tend to more closely incorporate with booming machine learning technologies, including deep learning approaches, for automatic feature extraction and description and for upgraded generalization performance. We introduce several new basic approaches on biometrics and machine learning in this book, and new propositions on applying machine learning algorithms to biometrics as well. We divided the book into two parts: Biometrics (Part I), and Machine Learning for Biometrics (Part II).

Part I "Biometrics" contains four chapters. Chapter 1 "Introduction" provides a brief and general introduction of the biometrics and machine learning. Chapter 2 "Recognition of Eye Characteristics" deals with the recognition of different types of information contained within the human eye, namely the iris and retina. Chapter 3 "Soft Biometrics" provides a holistic survey on soft biometrics that shows major works focusing on facial soft biometrics. It describes advanced techniques for feature extraction and classification that have been recently proposed and discusses the strengths and limitations of each technique. Chapter 4 "Face Recognition with Facial Occlusion Based on Local Cycle Graph Structure Operator" presents a local cycle graph structure (LCGS) operator for face recognition with facial occlusion.

Part II "Machine Learning for Biometrics" contains three chapters. Chapter 5 "Electrocardiogram Recognition Based on Variational Autoencoder" proposes a system to assist medical doctors by employing a technique based on variational autoencoder for automatic and fast estimation of the distortions. Chapter 6 "Survey on Methods of Image Processing and Recognition for Personal Identification" explores a survey of techniques on image processing and recognition for individual identification. Chapter 7 "A Human Body Mathematical Model Biometric Using Golden Ratio: A New Algorithm" provides more than 35-measurement rules derived from the perspectives of Vitruvian Man and Neufert and their basis of the golden proportion to build a human body model on computers.

The book is reviewed by editors: Prof. Jucheng Yang, Prof. Dong Sun Park, Prof. Sook Yoon, Dr. Yarui Chen, and Dr. Chuanlei Zhang.

Jucheng Yang, Yarui Chen, and Chuanlei Zhang
Tianjin University of Science and Technology
Tianjin, China

Dong Sun Park
Chonbuk National University
Jeonbuk, Republic of Korea

Sook Yoon
Mokpo National university
Jeonnam, Republic of Korea

Section 1

Biometrics

Chapter 1

Introductory Chapter: Machine Learning and Biometrics

Jucheng Yang, Yarui Chen, Chuanlei Zhang,
Dong Sun Park and Sook Yoon

Additional information is available at the end of the chapter

http://dx.doi.org/10.5772/intechopen.79346

1. Introduction

We are entering the era of artificial intelligence and big data, and thus, systems are becoming more intelligent with performance even to a human level in limited applications. We also connect every part of the globe with ultrahigh-speed Internet to share information in almost real time, and innovatively make changes on the life style of people. At the core of artificial intelligence, machine learning algorithms contribute to semiautomatically or automatically develop highly intelligent systems by overcoming existing difficulties for various fields including applications on engineering, business, science, and pure art.

Biometrics are emerging as essential technologies for Internet-era intelligent systems to ensure both computer and network securities as well as security for stand-alone equipment. To achieve a very high-level performance and more intelligent as intended, recent machine learning algorithms with state-of-the-art architectures can be applied to those biometric systems. In the book, we introduce some representative biometrics, discuss major characteristics of samples from corresponding biometric, and also describe their effective features and descriptors. We also introduce the well-known supervised machine learning algorithms and deep learning in separate chapters along with their applications to biometric studies.

2. Biometrics

Biometrics has rapidly developed in recent years with its worldwide applications for daily life. Biometrics authentication or recognition is to identify individuals based on the biometrics characteristics using a variety of types of algorithms [1]. Biometrics can be broadly categorized into two depending on their characteristics: physiological characteristics and behavioral characteristics. Biometrics with physiological characteristics contains direct physical evidence of discriminative features in their samples. This category includes biometrics such as face, fingerprints, palm veins, DNA, retina, iris, and ears. On the other hand, discriminative features from biometrics with behavioral characteristics can be indirectly extracted from samples, and this category includes biometrics such as typing rhythm, gait, and voice.

A biometric system for identification or recognition can be designed and implemented either feature-based using a handcrafted feature extraction or automatic feature generation-based using an end-to-end training based on a machine learning algorithm. For a feature-based biometric system, the selection of feature types and descriptors, and a following classifier design become very important to reduce the variability and the computational complexity of original characteristics. Each feature descriptor has its own strength for specific type of patterns. For example, the Gabor filter has better direction selectivity and frequency selectivity, so it can be used to apply time-frequency analysis for input images. Texture coding operators such as LBP and its variants are generally robust to changes from illumination and facial expression in images. Hence, it is critical to select right features according to the applications. Performance of a feature-based system mainly relies on capability of human experts, and it often results in low generalization for variations on input data. Recent automatic feature generation-based approaches such as deep learning can be an excellent alternative to deal with such difficulties. In this type of system, feature extraction/selection and classifier parts are trained together with large amount of data, and it generally shows better performance than a feature-based system. One disadvantage of this approach is that it usually consists of large number of parameters and takes a rather long time to train them.

Biometric systems for security require to have very high accuracy with favorably low computational complexity. In addition, a reliable biometric system should generalize well for unseen samples, and highly robust to various type of challenges including geometric transformation, illumination change, intraclass variation, and presence of noise. For a real-world security application, we need to construct a system endurable to various types of attacks such as counterfeiting. In order to make a system with higher security, multimodal biometrics [2] has attracted wide attentions in recent years and becomes a hot research topic. A multimodal system, for example, with input of finger vein and finger print images, has higher reliability, broader applicability, and stronger security and can provide a more reliable and stronger security in practical applications than unimodal one.

3. Machine learning

Machine learning is a procedure to learn from examples and, more specifically, it is a field of optimizing system parameters, which are defined on an architecture, to meet the evaluation criteria using a set of training examples. We often use statistical techniques to give computers the ability to "learn." Once the intended goal of learning is met, we may use the resulting system to automatically predict the category of unseen data, to estimate location in the feature space, or to generate artificial examples depending on different applications. Machine learning algorithms are typically classified into three broad categories: supervised learning, unsupervised learning, and reinforcement learning.

For supervised learning problems, the training data comprises examples of the input vectors along with their corresponding target vectors. When the target vectors are categorical, the problems are known as classification or pattern recognition, and when the target vectors are real-valued, the problems are known as regression. Loss or distance functions are defined between the current output vector and the target vector for each input vector, and optimization is performed to minimize the loss over all training examples. By teaching the system with known input and target pairs, we expect to respond correctly even if unseen data are presented to the trained system.

For unsupervised learning problems, no targets are defined so that the training data consist of only a set of input vectors. The goal of unsupervised learning is to automatically discover "interesting statistical structure" in the data. It can also be explained as latent knowledge discovery from examples, and a variety of clustering algorithms are canonical examples of unsupervised learning.

Reinforcement learning [3] is to learn how to act or behave in a given situation for given reward or penalty signals. In this type of learning, a state for current status is defined and environment, usually a criterion function, evaluates the current state to generate a proper reward or penalty action through a set of policies. Instead of having exact target values, it learns with critics.

Deep learning [4] has been inspired from human brain and has been proving its powerful ability in detection, classification, segmentation, key point estimation, to activity classification. It generally consists of huge number of parameters with multiple nonlinear layers. Deep learning architectures include two popular categories: convolutional neural networks (CNN) for automatic feature extraction and recurrent neural networks (RNN) for sequence estimation. They have been applied to computer vision, speech recognition, natural language processing, audio recognition, social network filtering, machine translation, and bioinformatics with outstanding performances. In addition, generative models such as variational encoders and generative adversarial networks (GAN) are also becoming popular with their artificial sample generation capability.

4. Conclusion

A biometric system for security should be very reliable and accurate. Feature-based biometric systems can be designed and implemented with their relatively high accuracy and fast response. For more reliable and accurate systems, machine learning techniques can be applied to biometrics and their application areas. Especially, novel powerful algorithms, such as deep learning algorithms, can be excellent candidates for solving the challenging biometrics problems.

Acknowledgements

This paper is supported by the National Natural Science Foundation of China under Grant No. 61502338.

Author details

Jucheng Yang[1]*, Yarui Chen[1], Chuanlei Zhang[1], Dong Sun Park[1,2] and Sook Yoon[3]

*Address all correspondence to: jcyang@tust.edu.cn

1 Tianjin University of Science and Technology, Tianjin, China

2 Chonbuk National University, Jeonbuk, Republic of Korea

3 Mokpo National University, Jeonnam, Republic of Korea

References

[1] Brunelli R, Falavigna D. Person identification using multiple cues. IEEE Transactions on Pattern Analysis and Machine Intelligence. 1995;**17**(10):955-966

[2] Yang J, Sun W, Liu N, Chen Y, Wang Y, Han S. A novel multimodal biometrics recognition model based on stacked ELM and CCA methods. Symmetry. 2018;**10**(4):96

[3] Mnih V, Kavukcuoglu K, Silver D, et al. Human-level control through deep reinforcement learning. Nature. 2015;**518**(7540):529

[4] Hinton GE, Salakhutdinov RR. Reducing the dimensionality of data with neural networks. Science. 2006;**313**(5786):504-507

Chapter 2

Recognition of Eye Characteristics

Martin Drahanský

Additional information is available at the end of the chapter

http://dx.doi.org/10.5772/intechopen.76026

Abstract

This chapter deals with the recognition of features contained within the human eye, namely the *iris* and *retina*. The great advantage is that both the iris and retina contain a large amount of information, that is, they can be used for a larger group of users. The disadvantage, on the other hand, is the fear from users in regard to possible eye injury. Both of these features cannot be easily acquired and misused to cheat a biometric system. This chapter also explains how to capture and process these two biometric characteristics. However, the number of biometric industrial solutions dealing with retina recognition is very limited—it is practically not possible to find an available biometric device for identity recognition on the market based on this biometric characteristic.

Keywords: eye characteristics, iris, retina, diseases, non-mydriatic fundus camera

1. Introduction

Just like the parts of our body mentioned earlier, our eyes are completely unique and can be used for biometric purposes. There are two core parts in our eyes that even show relatively high biometric entropy. The first is the eye iris and the second is the eye retina that lies inside the eye that is not observable by the naked eye of the observer. Recognition based on these two biometric characteristics is a relatively new industry. The first patent for automated iris recognition is from 1994 [1].

The iris and the retina as elements inside the eye are very well protected against damage. The iris and retina patterns are unique to every person (this also applies to monozygotic twins), although the structure and iris color are genetically dependent:

- The *cornea* is located at the front of the eye. It is a transparent connective tissue that, along with the lens, allows the light to break into the eye. Its bad curvature causes astigmatism.

- The *front chamber* is filled with intraocular fluid, which is constantly refreshed.
- The *iris* has the shape of an annulus, and it is a circularly arranged musculature that narrows/enlarges the pupil.
- The *pupil* is an opening in the middle of the iris, regulating the amount of light coming into the eye.
- The *lens* is suspended on the ciliary body and has the ability to bend and thereby change the refractive index. If the lens loses this ability, the eye cannot accommodate (focus).
- *Sclera* is a white visible layer covering the entire eyeball, which passes into the cornea in the front.
- The *vitreous* fluid fills the inside of the mesh.
- The *retina* is the inner part containing cells sensitive to light. It shows the image, much like a camera.
- The *optic nerve* carries a large number of nerve fibers that enter the central nervous system (CNS).

There are two scientific lines that deal with eye characteristics—those are *ophthalmology* and *biometrics*. *Ophthalmology* is a medical discipline aimed at analyzing and treating the health of the eye and its associated areas. The concept of *iridology* (the branch of alternative medicine that deals with the diagnosis of a person's health according to the image of the eye iris) is given only for completeness. In the field of *biometrics* (recognizing a person based on the unique biometric characteristics of the human body), the unique properties of the eye are not subject to change in time, and they are also so unique that it is possible to unequivocally identify two distinct individuals apart from each other in order to verify the identity of that person.

2. Recognition by iris

The *iris* is the colored part of the eye that we can see in others at a glance. The iris controls the amount of light that enters the eye, resembling a camera aperture that has the task of controlling the amount of light passing through the lens. The black hole in the center of the iris is called *pupil*. The iris is associated with fine muscles that either enlarges or narrows the iris. The color, texture, and pattern of the iris are different for each person, which is analogous to fingerprints, for example. However, the likelihood of finding two identical irises is much smaller than fingerprints.

The *clamping muscle* lies along the edge of the iris and pulls the iris in a stronger light. The *stretching muscle* lies transversely, similar to the bicycle strand, and stretches the iris when in dimmer illumination. The iris is flat and divides the eye into the front and back parts. **Figure 1** shows the anatomy of the human eye and the location of its individual parts.

The color of the iris is caused by a pigment called *melanin*. It is located between the pupil and the eye sclera. The size of the iris is about 11 mm. Its visual texture originates from the third month

http://dx.doi.org/10.5772/intechopen.76026

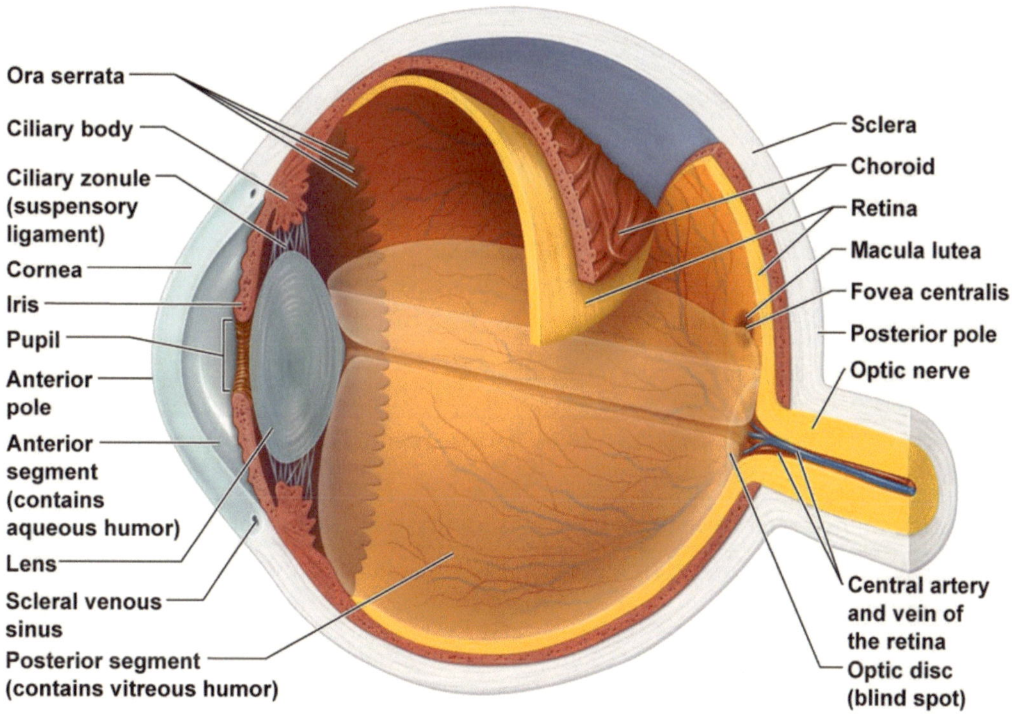

Figure 1. Anatomy of the human eye [2].

of pregnancy and forms during the first 2 years of life [4]. The basic structure remains unchanged during life, and even in twins, the iris is unique. The structure of the iris is shown in **Figure 2**.

The surface of the iris is quite complex. John Daugman described the 250 features that the iris contains. The most important of which for identification are the following:

- *Crypts*: atrophy in front and stroma forming its typical drawing; these are the thinnest places of the iris.
- *Radial furrows*: a series of very fine razor-shaped nibs extending from the pupil to the collar.
- *Pigment spots*: random clusters of pigment on the surface of the iris.

2.1. Influence of light on iris acquisition

The light we perceive around us is an electromagnetic waving in the visible spectrum. Each of these waves has its own wavelength. We see the colors as different wavelengths of the visible spectrum, but the eye responds to other wavelengths as well [5]:

- 100–315 nm: absorbed predominantly in the cornea, the rest is dispersed in ventricular water.
- 315–400 nm: absorbed in the lens.

- 400–1400 nm: passes through the lens on the retina. For visible light in the range of 400–700 nm, the eye reacts within 0.25 s.
- More than 1400 nm: it absorbs the cornea, causing strong tearing and increasing temperature.

Under the visible light, we can observe the visible layers, especially on the iris. It reveals less textural information than infrared (IR) light; melanin usually absorbs visible light.

By contrast, infrared (IR) light melanin predominantly reflects and is preferred for iris recognition because it is more user-friendly; it does not irritate and does not cause the unpleasant feelings associated with eye illumination.

There are four basic schemes for iris recognition:

- *Gabor demodulation*: each single pattern on the iris is demodulated to obtain phase information for the extraction of features [6].
- *Wavelet features*: extract the vector of features using wavelet transform [7].
- *Analysis of independent components*: independent component analysis factors [8] are used as a vector of features.
- *Local keys variation*: representations of important information by the set of intensities of one-dimensional signals, using wavelet transformation for the extraction of features [9].

2.2. Gabor's demodulation (Daugman's algorithm)

The first step of Gabor's demodulation, or Daugman's algorithm, is to locate the iris in the acquired image. The iris must be properly scanned so that it can be mapped into phase diagrams that carry information about the position, orientation, and number of specific identification features. After extraction, the database is searched for the template. Daugman's algorithm is shown in **Figure 3**.

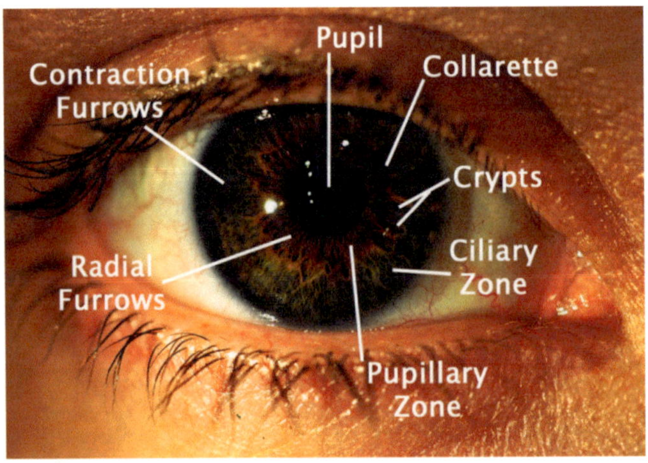

Figure 2. Structure of the iris—features [3].

First, an *iris* (curve boundary) is *located* in the image of the eye. The iris is located with the following operator:

$$\max_{(r,x_0,y_0)}\left|G_\sigma(r) * \frac{\partial}{\partial r}\oint_{r,x_0,y_0}\frac{I(x,y)}{2\pi r}ds\right| \tag{1}$$

where $G_\sigma(r)$ is the Gaussian smoothing function according to σ, $I(x,y)$ is the raw input image, and the operator searches for the maximum in the blurred partial derivative of the image with respect to the radius r and the center coordinates (x_0, y_0). The operator is essentially a circular edge detector and returns the maximum if the candidate circle shares the pupil center and the radius. Examples of localized irises are shown in **Figure 4**.

The next step is *locating* the *lid*. The position of the lower and upper eyelids is determined by the same procedure as the iris itself. The part of the previous formula (Eq. (1)) used to detect the contour is replaced by a circular arc, the parameters being set according to standard

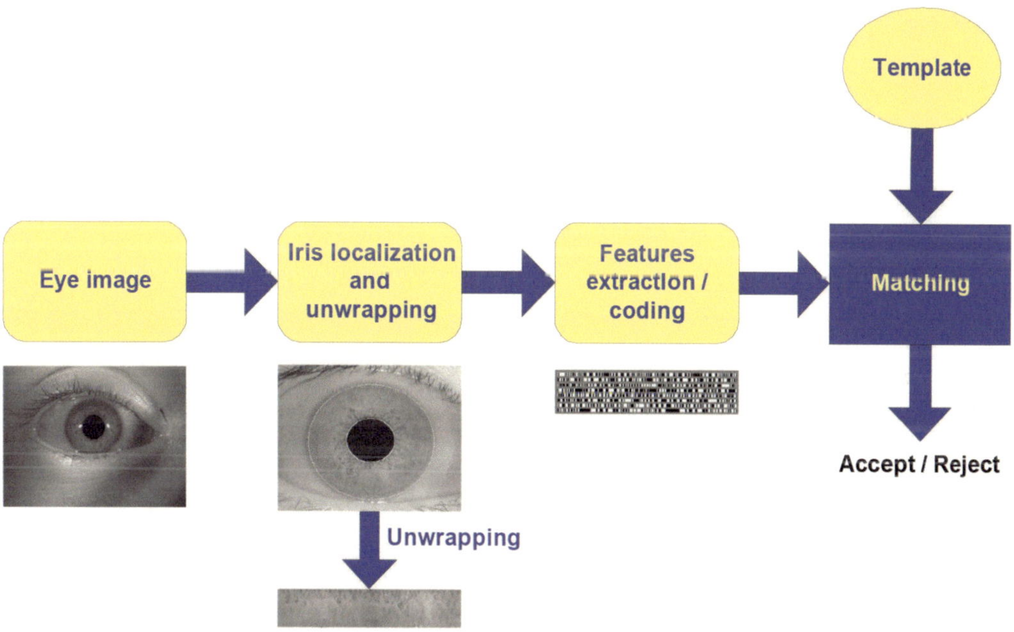

Figure 3. Identification process of Daugman's algorithm.

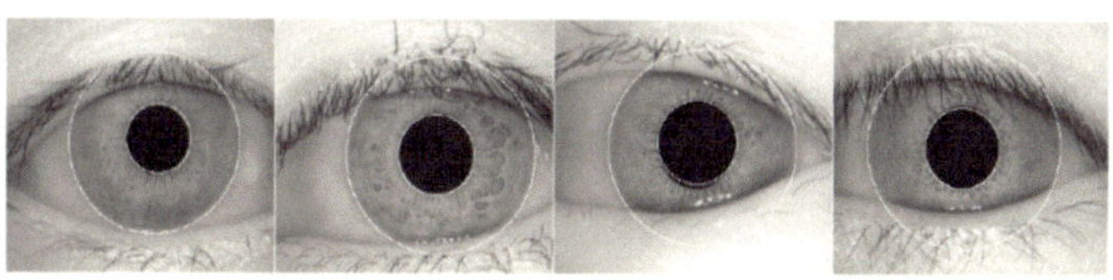

Figure 4. Examples of localized irises.

statistical estimation methods to optimally correspond to each eyelid boundary. An example of localized lids is shown in **Figure 5**.

2.3. Daugman's gross alignment model

Daugman's gross alignment model maps each point within the iris to the polar coordinates (r, θ) where r is from the interval $\langle 0, 1 \rangle$ and θ is the angle from the interval $\langle 0, 2n \rangle$.

The model compensates the pupil enlargement and dilatation due to the representation in the polar coordinate system, invariant to size and translation. However, the model does not compensate for rotational inconsistency, which is solved by shifting the iris template in the direction of the θ at the comparison stage until both templates reach a match. The introduction of the coordinate system is shown in **Figure 6**.

2.4. Iris features encoding

Gabor filtering in the polar coordinate system is defined as

$$G(r, \theta) = e^{j\omega(\theta-\theta_0)} e^{-\frac{(r-r_0)^2}{\alpha^2}} e^{-\frac{j(\theta-\theta_0)^2}{\beta^2}} \tag{2}$$

where (r, θ) indicates the position in the image, (α, β) determine the effective height and length, and ω is the frequency of the filter. Demodulation and phase quantification are expressed as

$$g_{\{\mathrm{Re,Im}\}} = \mathrm{sgn}_{\{\mathrm{Re,Im}\}} \iint_{\rho\phi} I(\rho, \phi)\, e^{j\omega(\theta_0-\phi)}\, e^{-\frac{(r_0-\rho)^2}{\alpha^2}}\, e^{-\frac{(\theta_0-\phi)^2}{\beta^2}}\, \rho d\rho d\varphi \tag{3}$$

where $I(r, \phi)$ is the rough iris image in the polar coordinate system, and $g_{\{Re,Im\}}$ is a bit in the complex plane corresponding to the sign of the real and imaginary part of the filter response. **Figure 7** shows the coding process of the iris.

The iris code contains 2048 bits (256 bytes). The size of the input image is 64 × 256 bytes, the iris code size is 8 × 32 bytes, and the Gabor filter size is 8 × 8. An example of the iris code is shown in **Figure 8**.

2.5. Comparison of iris codes

The comparison is made by calculating the Hamming distance between the two 256 dwelling codes. The Hamming distance between iris codes A and B is given as the sum of exclusive totals (XOR) between bits:

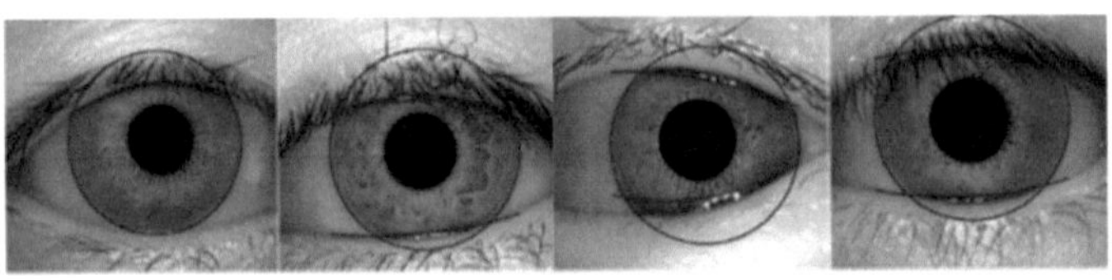

Figure 5. Examples of localized lids.

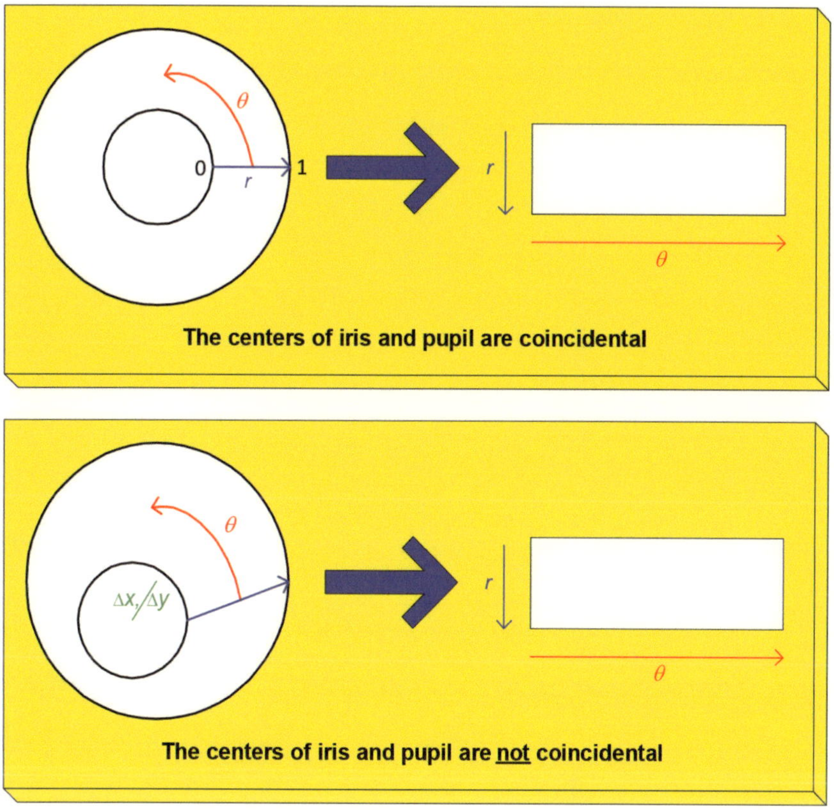

Figure 6. Implementation of Daugman's algorithm coordinate system.

$$HD = \frac{1}{N}\sum_{j=1}^{N} A_j \otimes B_j \tag{4}$$

where $N = 2048\ (8 \times 256)$, unless the iris is shaded by the lid. Otherwise, only valid areas are used to calculate the Hamming distance.

If both samples are obtained from the same iris, the Hamming distance between them is equal to or close to zero (due to the high correlation of both samples). To ensure rotational consistency, one pattern is shifted to the right/left and the corresponding Hamming distance is always calculated. The lowest value of the Hamming distance is then taken as the resultant comparison score. An example of how to compare iris codes using shifts is shown in **Figure 9**.

2.6. The advantages and disadvantages of the iris for biometric identification

Some *advantages* of using an iris for biometric identification systems are the following:

- The iris is stable during an individual's life.
- Snapshots are noninvasive and user-friendly.

- The size of the template is small.
- The iris is an internal organ that is relatively well protected against external influences.
- The iris has a high level of biometric entropy information, much larger than fingerprints.

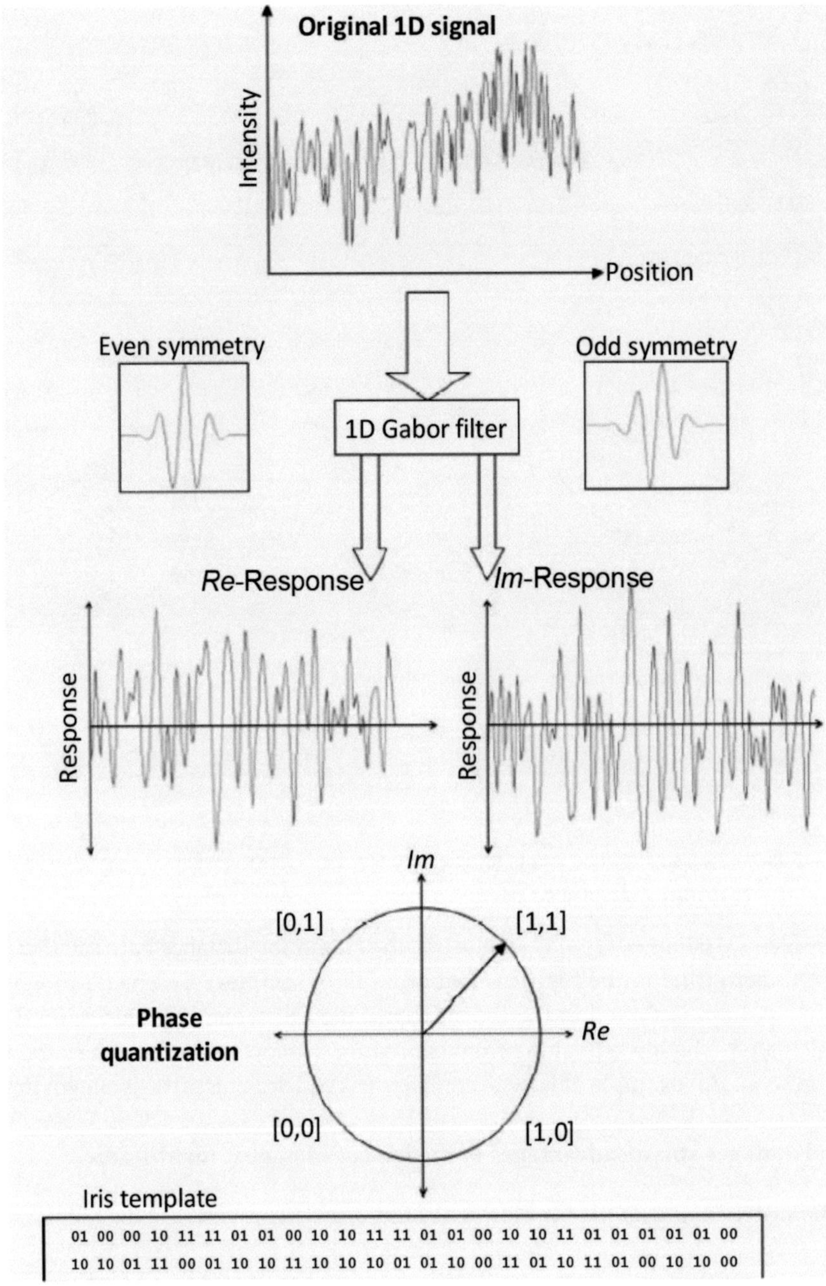

Figure 7. Illustration of the encoding process.

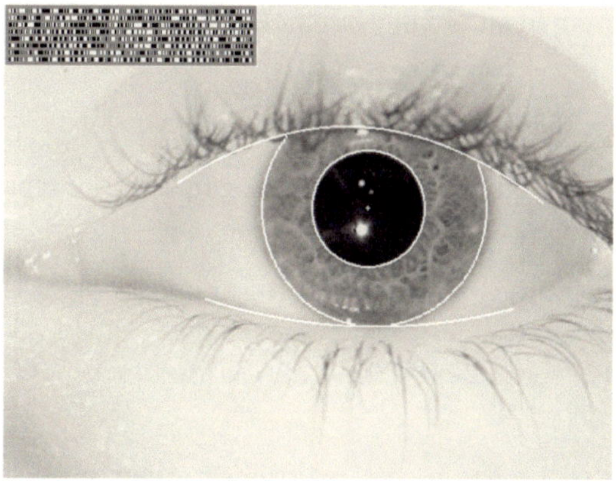

Figure 8. Example of an iris code.

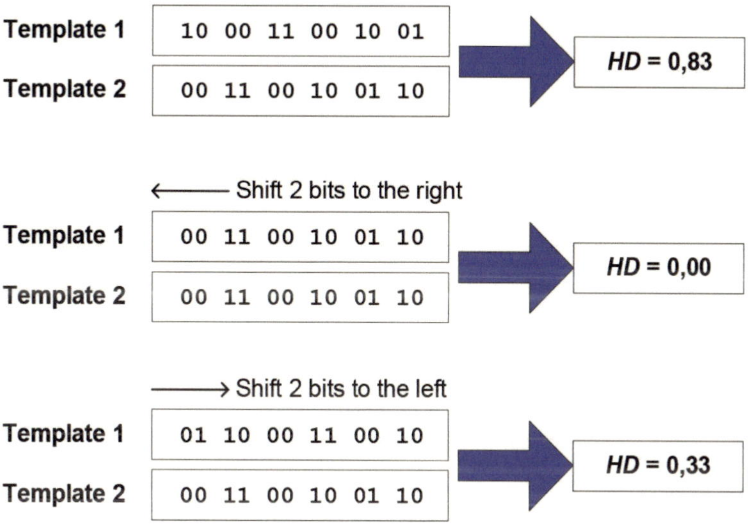

Figure 9. Example of the comparison of iris codes using shifts.

The *disadvantages* of using the iris for recognition are as follows:

- The lack of a system to counter against a photograph of an iris (spoofing) or contact lenses.
- Obstruction may also be the prejudice of users who believe that the scanner may damage the eye.

The following list summarizes the limitations of iris recognition. In a way, it is possible to include them among the disadvantages:

- The acquisition of an iris image requires user collaboration; the user must stand at a predetermined distance and position in front of the camera. Some systems already allow a semi-automatic scanning to automatic, but the error rate of these systems is still relatively high.

- Relatively high cost for high-performance systems.
- Images of the iris may be of poor quality, resulting in errors in registration, verification, or identification.
- The iris can change over time, especially due to various illnesses. Changing the iris is possible in cataract surgery and illnesses such as *nystagmus* (shaking eyes) or *aniridia* (a completely missing iris). For some blind people, the iris may not be visible at all due to clouding of the eyes.
- The individual parts of the iris are related to the various internal organs of the human body, resulting in the possibility of misusing the scanned pattern to determine the health of the person. This alternative medicine area is called *iridology* [10].

3. Recognition by retina

Recognition by the retina is another option offered by the eye. Perhaps, the most complicated part of the entire retinal identification procedure is to obtain a good-quality eye image. Here, it is possible to inspire the principles of medical devices for the examination of an eye. It is also necessary to understand the function of the retina for human vision, its location, and the elements contained therein, according to which biometric identification can be carried out.

3.1. Anatomy of the retina

The retina is considered to be a part of the *central nervous system* (CNS). This is the only part of the CNS that can be observed noninvasively. It is a light-sensitive layer of cells located at the back of the eye with a thickness of 0.2–0.4 mm. It is responsible for sensing the light rays that hit it through the pupil and an eye lens that turns and inverts the image. The retina is a complex structure with several layers of neurons linked by synapses (**Figure 10**). The only neurons that react directly to light are *photoreceptors*. These are divided into two main types: *cones* and *rods*. In adults, the retina covers approximately 72% of the inner eye. The entire surface of the retina contains about 7 million cones and 75–150 million rods. This would compare the eye to a 157 MP camera. Rods are used to detect light and are capable of responding to the impact of one to two photons by providing black and white vision. Cones are used to detect colors and are divided into three types depending on which base color they are sensitive to (red, green, blue), but these are less sensitive to light intensity. In these cells, there is a phenomenon called *transduction* where the cascade of chemical and electrical phenomena changes into electrical impulses. These are then transmitted through the optic nerve to the central nervous system.

We can observe the two most distinctive points on an eye's retina. It is a *blind spot* (or an optical disc) and a *macula* (*yellow spot*). A blind spot is the point where the optic nerve enters the

http://dx.doi.org/10.5772/intechopen.76026

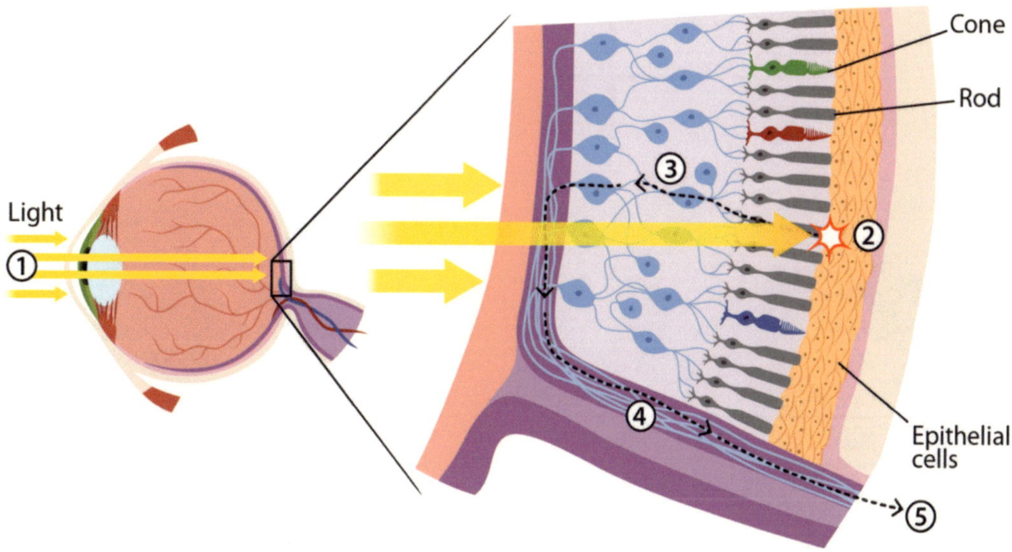

Figure 10. Structure of the retina [11].

eye, has a size of about 3 mm^2, and lacks all receptors. So, if the image falls into the blind spot, it will not be visible to a person. The brain often "guesses" how the image should look in order to fill this place. The existence of a blind spot can be tested as shown in **Figure 11**. If we close the left eye and observe the cross, then the black circle disappears at a certain distance from the image. This is precisely the moment when this image lands on a blind spot [5].

On the other hand, the *macula* (*yellow spot*) is referred to as the sharpest vision area, has a diameter of about 5 mm, and the cones predominate it (it is less sensitive to light). This area has the highest concentration of light-sensitive cells whose density is decreasing toward the edges. The center of the macula is *fovea*, which is the term describing receptor concentration and visual acuity. Our direct view is reflected in this area. Interestingly enough, the macula (yellow spot) is not really yellow, but slightly redder than the surrounding area. This attribute, however, was given by the fact that yellow appears after the death of an individual.

The retina is nourished by the *choroid*, which is a layer located between the retina and the sclera. It contains blood vessels and a pigment absorbing excess light. **Figure 12** shows how the retina is richly interwoven with nourishing vessels and nerves. It shows a similar apparatus to the brain, where the structure and venous tangle remain unchanged throughout life. The retina has two main sources of blood supply—the retinal artery and vessels. Larger blood flow to the retina is through the blood vessel that nourishes its outer layer with photoreceptors. Another blood supply is provided by the retinal artery, which primarily nourishes the inside of the retina. This artery usually has four major branches.

The retina located inside the eye is well protected from external influences. During life, the vessel pattern does not change and is therefore suitable for biometric purposes.

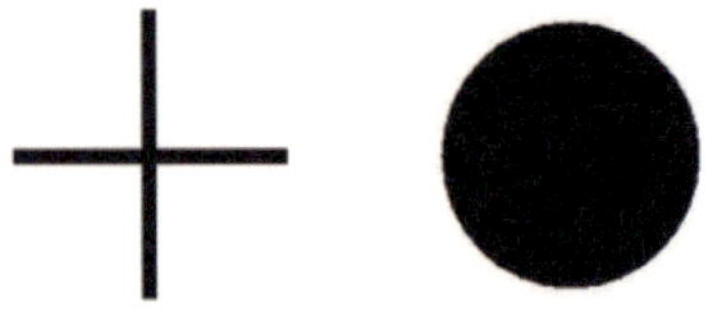

Figure 11. Blind spot testing.

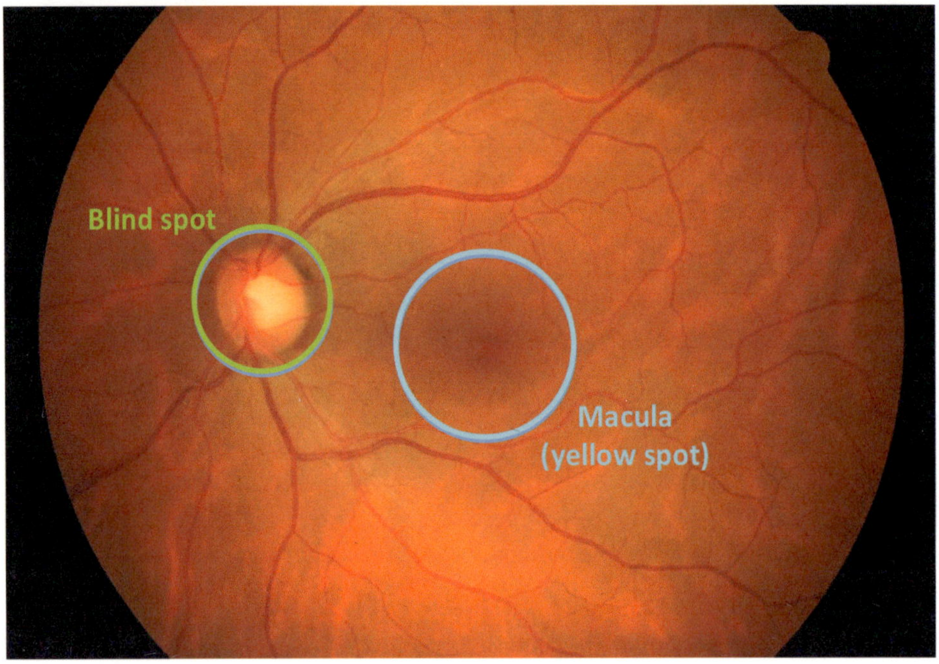

Figure 12. A snapshot of the retina taken by the fundus camera.

The retina acquires an image similar to a camera. The beam passing through the pupil appears in the focus of the lens on the retina, much like film. In medical practice, specialized optical devices are used for the visual examination of the retina.

3.2. Eye diseases

In the field of ophthalmology, the iris is not very interesting because when we neglect the extreme and very rare cases of a disease (e.g., irrigation or perforation of the iris, irritation of the iris), pigment changes occur often, which is not the result of a disease and has no effect on human health. The main focus is on ophthalmology in regard to examining the retina of the eye, of course taking into account the overall health of the eye (e.g., cataracts or increased intraocular pressure). In the retina, there is a relatively large line of diseases and damage that interest medical doctors, but they are detailed in an encyclopedia of ophthalmology with hundreds of pages (e.g., [12] (1638 pages) or [13] (2731 pages)). The large group is diabetes and age-related macular degeneration (ARMD). Occasionally, exudates/druses or hemorrhages (bleeding or blood clots) appear in the retina; however, as mentioned earlier, potential damage (e.g., perforation or retinal detachment) or retinal disease is such a matter to go to ophthalmologists. Since our research group works with medical doctors, we process images or video sequences in which we look for pathological manifestations. At the present time, we focus on detecting and delimiting the exudates/druses and hemorrhages in the image, automatically detecting the position of the macula and blind spot. These are the reference points by which we determine the location of pathological findings. The worst area is the part called the fovea centralis, where the sharpest vision is located. Once this area is damaged, it has a very significant impact on our sight. An example of the detection of pathological findings is shown in **Figure 13**. We also deal with colleagues by detecting the quality of blood flow in the retina. There is still much to do in all areas of imaging and video processing for medical purposes, as input data are very different. For the time being (and probably still remaining so for a long time), the best diagnostic tool is a medical doctor.

Every part of the human body can be affected by a disease, whether it's curable or not. An incurable disease will be understood as a disability that cannot be surgically or otherwise removed without the biometric information (e.g., amputation) disappearing. The curable disease is removable with minimal consequences (e.g., inflammation, cuts). The retina can be affected by both types of these diseases. These diseases can significantly affect the course of recognition. If a disease disrupts the structure of the retina, it may cause erroneous evaluation or a complete rejection of the pattern.

3.2.1. Macular degeneration

Macular degeneration is a disease that occurs in 90% of cases with age, also known as aged-related macular degeneration (ARMD). In the remaining percentage, macular degeneration occurs in children or young people in the form of *Best's macular degeneration* or *Stargardt's disease*. These diseases arise on the basis of inheritance.

In macular degeneration, the area of the retina, which forms at the center of the field of vision, is violated (**Figure 14**). As a result, a major disturbance of the central field of vision arises. In the center, the patient sees a gray shadow down to a black spot. The peripheral vision of the

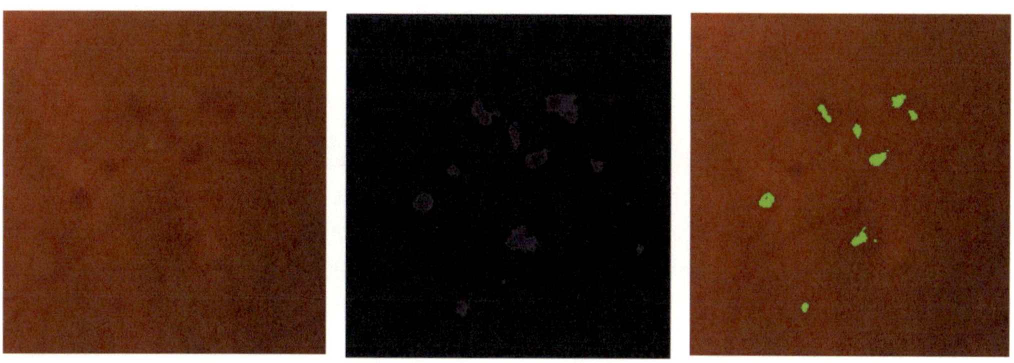

Figure 13. Hemorrhage (left), detection of suspected areas (center), and highlighted hemorrhage (right).

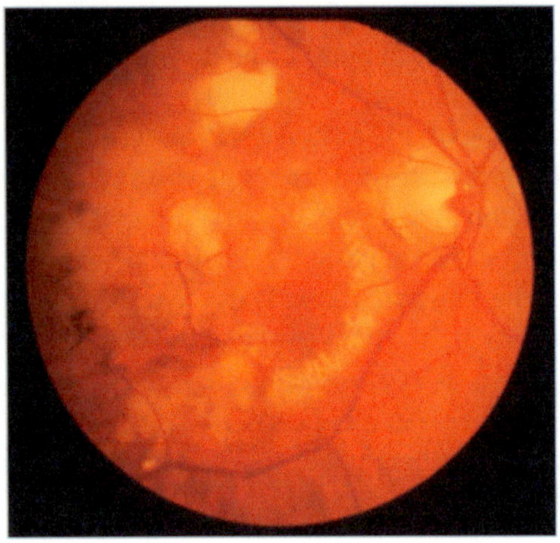

Figure 14. Macular degeneration.

macula remains intact. Macular degeneration can occur in two forms of dry (*atrophic*) and wet (*exudative*). The most common symptoms include a blurred gray or a black spot at the center of the field of vision (the so-called *central scotoma*). The affected person sees deformed straight lines, blurred letters, or inappropriate shapes of different objects. It also affects color vision, which seems to have faded. Side vision remains sharp on one or both eyes [14].

3.2.2. Diabetic retinopathy

Diabetic retinopathy (DR) is an inflammatory disease of the retina. It arises as a result of the total affection of blood vessels in diabetes mellitus. Wrongly diagnosed diabetes affects small catheters that clog in the eyes, causing blood circulation to slow. The second way the retina is affected is that the vessels "leak" and the fluid escapes and causes the retina to swell. Insufficient blood circulation and swelling of the retina destroy vision. The eye tries to remedy the situation by growing new blood vessels (*neovascularization*), but they are poor and harmful, they crack, they can bleed in the eye (*hemophthalmos*), and they can cause traction detachment of the retina. Diabetic retinopathy has two forms: *non-proliferative* and *proliferative* [15] (**Figure 15**).

3.2.3. Toxoplasmosis

Toxoplasmosis is a disease that ranks among *zoonoses*, which is transmissible from animals to humans. It occurs all over the world. In European countries, anti-toxoplasmosis antibodies are produced by 10–60% of the population depending on dietary habits. In the Czech Republic, *seropositivity* (the presence of antibodies in the blood) is around 20–40%. Diseases are most often manifested by elevated temperatures, flu-like conditions, headaches, fatigue, or swollen lymph nodes. An acute infection may sometimes go into a chronic stage, but the infection is often unnoticed and is only recognized by the finding of specific anti-toxoplasmic antibodies in the blood, which may persist in low levels throughout their lives (the latent form

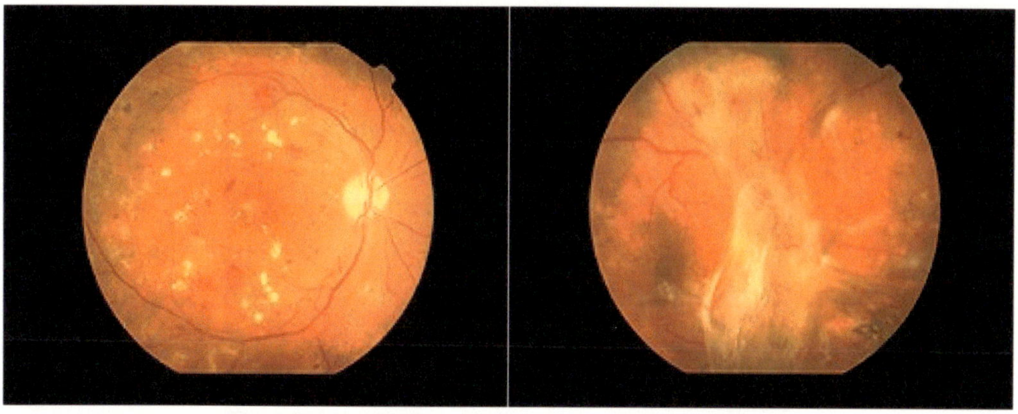

Figure 15. Non-proliferative (left) and proliferative diabetic retinopathy.

of infection). There are many forms of illness—nodal, ocular (see **Figure 16**), cerebral, gynecological. The other forms of toxoplasmosis are uncommon [16].

3.3. Retinal examination tools

The most commonly used device for examining the retina is a *direct ophthalmoscope*. When using an ophthalmoscope, the patient's eye is examined from a distance of several centimeters through the pupil. Several types of ophthalmoscopes are currently known but the principle is essentially the same: the eye of the investigated and the investigator is in one axis, and the retina is illuminated by a light source from a semipermeable mirror or a mirror with a hole located in the observation axis at an angle of 45° [17]. The disadvantage of a direct ophthalmoscope is a relatively small area of investigation, the need for skill when handling, and patient cooperation.

For a more thorough examination of the eye background, the so-called *fundus camera*, which is currently most likely to have the greatest importance in examining the retina, is used. It allows color photography to make up virtually the entire surface of the retina, as can be seen in **Figure 12**. The optical principle of this device is based on the so-called indirect ophthalmoscopy [17]. Fundus cameras are equipped with a white light source to illuminate the retina and then scan it with a charge-coupled device (CCD) sensor. Some types can also find the center of the retina and automatically focus it using a frequency analysis of the scanned image.

3.4. Histology of retinal recognition

In 1935, ophthalmologists *Carleton Simon* and *Isidore Goldstein* discovered eye diseases where the image of the bloodstream in two individuals in the retina was unique for each individual. Subsequently, they published a journal article on the use of vein image in the retina as a unique pattern for identification [18]. Their research was supported by Dr. Paul Tower, who in 1955 published an article on studying monozygotic twins [19]. He discovered that retinal

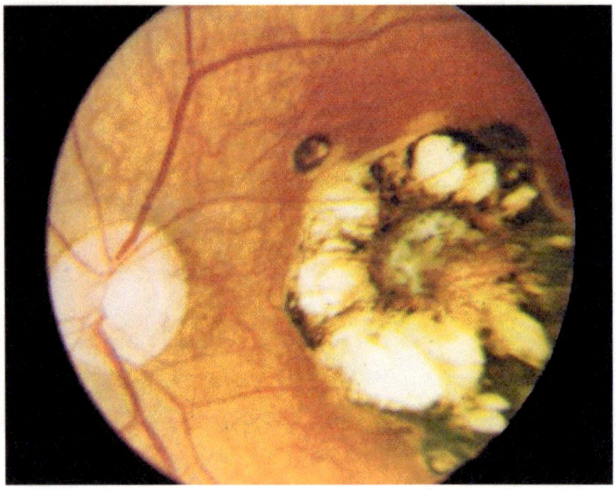

Figure 16. Eye affected by toxoplasmosis.

vessel patterns show the least resemblance to all the other patterns examined. At that time, identification of the vessel's retina was a timeless thought.

With the concept of a simple fully automated device capable of retrieving a snapshot of the retina and verifying the identity of the user, *Robert Hill,* who established *EyeDentify* in 1975, devoted almost all of his time and effort to the development. However, functional devices did not appear on the market for several years.

Several other companies attempted to use the available fundus cameras and modify them to retrieve the image of the retina for identification purposes. However, these fundus cameras had several significant disadvantages, such as the relatively complicated alignment of the optical axis, visible light spectra, making the identification quite uncomfortable for the users, and last but not least, the cost of these cameras were very high.

Further experiments led to the use of infrared (IR) illumination, as these beams are almost transparent to the choroid that reflects this radiation to create an image of eye blood vessels. IR illumination is invisible to humans, so there is also no reduction in the pupil diameter when the eye is irradiated.

The first working prototype of the device was built in 1981. The device with an eye-optic camera used to illuminate the IR radiation was connected to an ordinary personal computer for image capture analysis. After extensive tests, a simple correlation comparison algorithm was chosen as the most appropriate.

After another 4 years of hard work, EyeDentify Inc. launched the *EyeDentificationSystem 7.5,* where verification is performed based on the retina image and the PIN entered by the user with the data stored in the database.

The device performed a circular snapshot of the retina. The image consisted of 256 twelve-bit logarithmic samples reduced to a reference record of 40 bytes for each eye. Contrast information is stored in the time domain. In addition, 32 bytes were added per each eye in the time domain to accelerate recognition.

3.5. Technology and principles

The functional principle of the device can be divided into three non-trivial subsystems [20]:

- *Image, signal acquisition, and processing*: the optical system and the camera must be capable of capturing a digital image of the retina suitable for processing.
- *Comparison*: a program on a device or a computer that extracts key features from a scanned image and compares it to a database of patterns.
- *Representation*: each retinal image must be represented in such a way that it can be quickly compared or stored in the database.

3.5.1. Sensing optical system

Now, we introduce sensing devices that are used to capture images of the front or the back of the eye. The main ophthalmoscopic examination methods of the anterior and posterior parts of the eye include direct and indirect ophthalmoscopy as well as the most widely used examination, a *slit lamp* (see **Figure 17** on the left), which makes it possible to examine the anterior segment of the eye using the so-called *biomicroscopy*. *Fundus camera*, sometimes referred to as a *retinal camera*, is a special device for displaying the posterior segment of the optic nerve eye, the yellow spots, and the peripheral part of the retina (see **Figure 17** on the right). It works on the principle of indirect ophthalmoscopy where a source of primary white light is built inside the instrument. The light can be modified by different types of filters, and the optical system is focused on the patient's eye, where it reflects from the retina and points back to the fundus camera lens. There are mydriatic and non-mydriatic types that differ in whether or not the patient's eye must be taken into

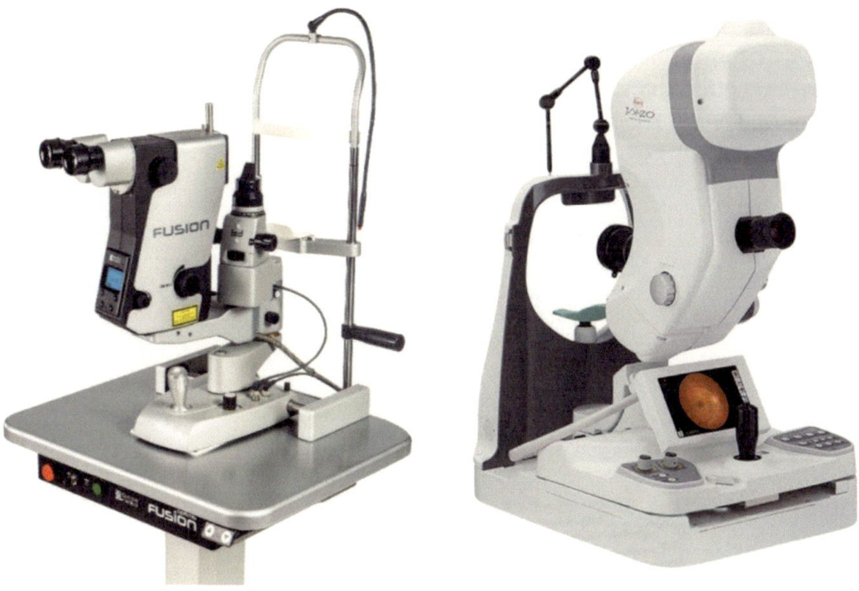

Figure 17. (left) Slit lamp example [21] and (right) example of a non-mydriatic fundus camera [22].

mydriasis. The purpose of mydriasis is to extend the human eye's pupil so that the "inlet opening" is larger allowing one to be able to read a larger part of the retina. Certainly, non-mydriatic fundus cameras are preferred because the patient can immediately leave after the examination and can drive a motor vehicle, which is not possible in the case of mydriasis. However, in some patients, mydriasis is necessary. The price of these medical devices is in the order of tens of thousands of Euros, which is determined only by medical specialized workplaces.

The mechanical construction of the optical device is a rather complex matter. It is clear that the scanning device operates on the principle of medical eye-optic devices. These so-called retinoscopes, or fundus cameras, are relatively complicated devices, and the price for them is high as well.

The principle is still the same as for a retinoscope, where a beam of light is focused on the retina, and the CCD camera scans the reflected light. The beam of light from the retinoscope is adjusted so that the eye lens focuses on the surface of the retina. This reflects a portion of the transmitted light beam back to the ophthalmic lens that then readjusts it, the beam leaving the eye at the same angle below which the eye enters (return reflection). In this way, an image of the surface of the eye can be obtained at about 10° around the visual axis, as shown in **Figure 18**. The device performed a circular snapshot of the retina, mainly due to the reflection of light from the cornea, which would be unusable during raster scanning.

The first products from EyeDentify used a relatively complicated optical system with rotating mirrors to cover the area of the retina—this system is described in U.S. Pat. No. 4,620,318 [23]. To align the scan axis and the visual axis, the so-called UV-IR cut filters (*Hot Mirrors*—reflects infrared light and passes through the visible light) are used in the design. A schematic drawing of the patent is shown in **Figure 19**. The distance between the eye and the lens was about 2–3 cm from the camera. The alignment system on the optical axis of the instrument is an important issue, and it is described in more detail in U.S. Pat. No. 4,923,297 [24].

Newer optical systems from EyeDentify are much easier and have the benefits of fixing optical axes with less user effort than the previous systems. The key part is a rotating scanning disc that carries multifocal Fresnel lenses. This construction is described in U.S. Pat. No. 5,532,771 [25].

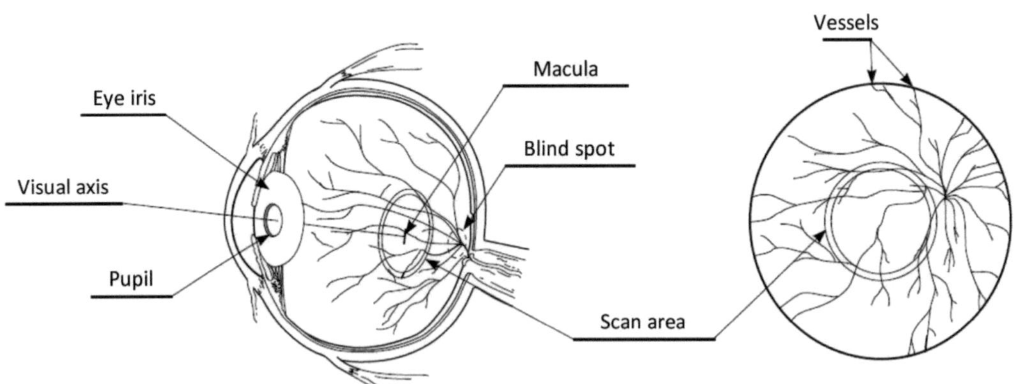

Figure 18. Functional principle for obtaining a retinal image of the eye background.

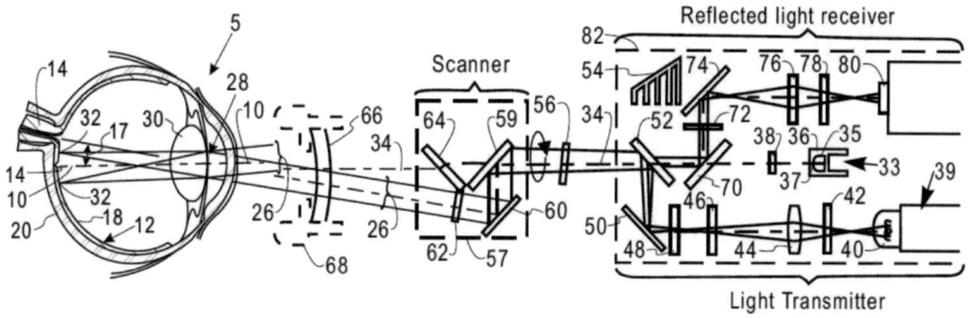

Figure 19. The first version of EyeDentificationSystem 7.5 optical system.

To ensure that the area is focused on the retina and that the eye of the user is in the axis of the scanning beam, the fixation point/target must be approximately in that same position throughout the scanning period. This can be a range of optical networks with focal distances of −7, −3, 0, and +3 diopters. It is expected that most users will be able to focus regardless of their optical defects. When the eye focuses on a target, the device automatically aligns itself to the axis by centering the rotating disc to the eye background. If a user aligns two or more optical patterns behind each other, the IR beam is centered on his or her pupil and the information can be read.

3.5.2. Comparison

Whenever a user looks into the camera's optical system, their head may be rotated slightly different from the original scanned position. The rotary algorithm (phase corrector) can rotate the data by several degrees. This process takes place several times until the best match is reached, that is, the highest correlation.

Comparison of the obtained samples is ensured in several steps:

- Using sampling, the eye reference is converted into a field with the same number of elements as the field obtained, which ensures alignment (sample overlay).
- Both fields are normalized so that RMS is equal to 1, normalizing the intensity.
- The field is correlated using a Fourier transform equivalent time domain.

The comparator quality is given by the correlation value where the time shift is zero. It is in the range of +1 (absolute match) to −1 (absolute mismatch). Experience has shown that a score of around 0.7 can be considered a match.

3.5.3. Representation

The retinal representation is derived from a frame composed of annular regions (EyeDentificationSystem 7.5 operates on a circular scanning principle). The size of the scanned area is selected for the worst possible scanning conditions (very small pupil) but is also sufficient for biometric identification. For these purposes, it is not necessary to obtain an image with too much area and resolution.

In connection with a device from EyeDentify, there were two main representations of the retinal image:

- The original representation has 40 bytes. This is contrast information encoded by real and imaginary spectrum coordinates generated by Fourier transform.
- The new representation has 48 bytes. This does not contain time domain contrast information. The main advantage of time representation is faster and more efficient processing with less demanding computing power.

The retina template contains 96 fields of 4-bit contrast numbers from 96 scans of concentric circles in the time domain, that is, 96 × 4 = 48 bytes. Intensity in the time range can take values in the interval <–8.7>, normalizing for this layout—4 bits of intensive layout.

In the retina, when we talk about new research, the situation is relatively simple because the algorithms are searching the image for *bifurcations* and *crossings*, whose positions clearly define the person. The example is shown in **Figure 20**. Recognition becomes problematic when a stronger pathological phenomenon (e.g., a hemorrhage) occurs in the retina that affects the detection

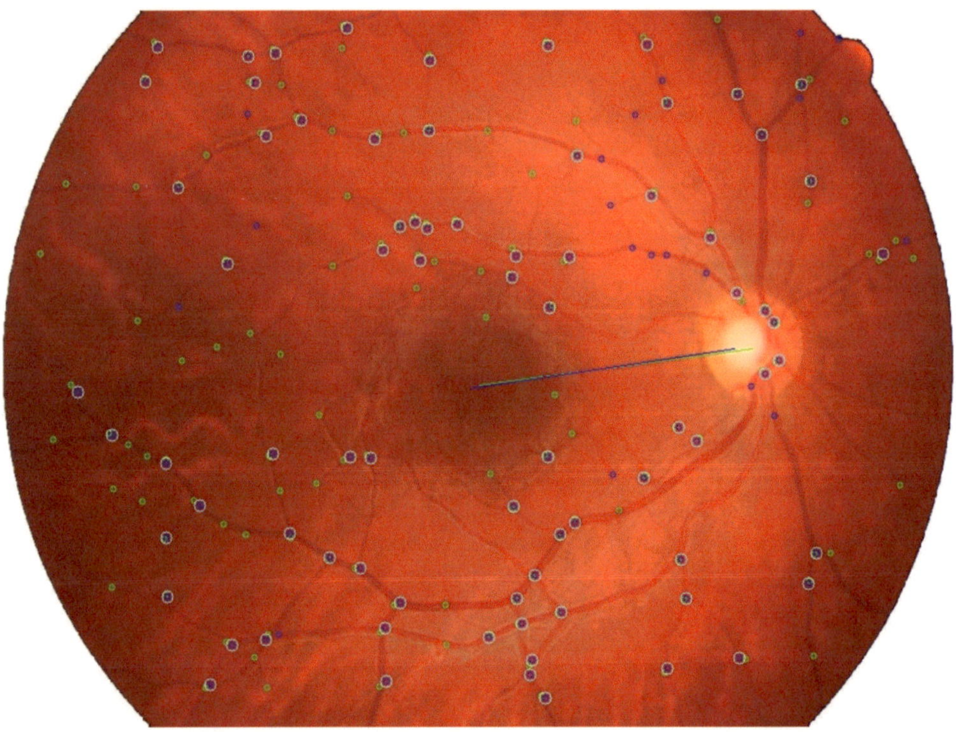

Figure 20. Extracted features (bifurcations and crossings, incl. connection of macula and blind spot) in the retina.

and extraction of bifurcations and crossings. For biometric systems, it should be noted that their use also includes the disclosure of information about their own health status since, as mentioned earlier, a relatively large amount of information on human health can be read from the image of an iris, and that is especially so from a retina as well. It is therefore up to each of us on how much we will protect this private information and whether or not we will use the systems. However, if the manufacturer guarantees that the health information does not get stored, and only the unique features are stored (not the image), then we all may be more than happy to use the system.

3.6. Limitations

Of popular biometrics, retinal recognition may be the most restrictive. They are not definite, but there is currently no system that can remove these shortcomings to a greater extent [20]:

- *Fear of eye damage*: the low level of IR illumination used in this type of device is completely harmless to the eye, but there is a myth among the lay public that these devices can damage the retina. All users need to be familiar with the system in order to gain confidence.
- *Outdoor and indoor use*: small pupils can increase the false reject rate. Since the light has to pass through the pupil twice (once in the eye, second outwards), the return beam can be significantly weakened if the user's pupil is too small.
- *Ergonomics*: the need to come in close to the sensor may reduce the comfort of using the device more than other biometric methods.
- *Severe astigmatism*: people with visual impairment (astigmatism) are unable to focus the eye onto the point (a function comparable to measuring the focusing ability of the eye for an ophthalmologist), thus avoiding the correct generation of the template.
- *High price*: it can be assumed that the price of the device, especially the retroviral optical device itself, will always be greater than, for example, the price of fingerprint or voice recognition devices.

4. Characteristics of iris and retina recognition technology

In the subsequent subsection, we discuss the iris and retinal recognition characteristics. Some of the characteristics already arise from the previous subsections where the principles of sensing and processing these biometric features have been described.

4.1. Acceptance

4.1.1. Iris

The acceptance for iris identification is on a middle level because there is no need for immediate interaction with the user. The user only has to stand in front of the device and look toward the sensor at a certain distance without rotating the head. The image capture and evaluation time is about 2 s.

4.1.2. Retina

In the case of the retina, the acceptance rate is low. Many people are afraid of using this technology. They are convinced that a laser will be used that could harm their eye. However, these concerns are totally unnecessary because a laser is never used in this case. Another problem is the retinal image retrieval procedure itself. This is tedious, which can be uncomfortable for some users.

For the retina, a direct user interaction is also required (to be close to the device (centimeter distance) and focus on the fixation points). At least with the current methods, there must be a relatively large cooperation by the user. Acceptance is therefore low.

4.2. Reliability

4.2.1. Iris

When scanning the image of an iris, it is possible to obtain insufficient eye information due to ambient light, eyelids being too closed, and so on. However, this is a fairly reliable identification method.

The accuracy of the comparison of the two iris patterns is represented by the so-called Hamming distance, that is, the number of bits in which the comparison of two different iris patterns differs. It is reported that for the probability of an incorrect comparison of 1:26,000,000, the Hamming distance is 0.32 (i.e., only about one-third of the identical bits of the two patterns).

Figure 21 shows the distribution of Hamming's distance when comparing the high number of irises [26]. The graph is a binomial distribution with a probability of 0.5. It also follows from the graph that it is highly unlikely that two different irises differ in less than one-third of the information.

4.2.2. Retina

Regarding retinal scanning, its reliability is high. However, there are conditions where it is not possible to obtain a sufficiently good image of the retina. In particular, it is bad illumination—the user has a heavily closed pupil when scanning due to the large amount of light. Another problem occurs with the abovementioned diseases or other dysfunctions of the eye.

Recognition by the retina is not very widespread, perhaps because there are not really many objective tests of this method. In 1991, the international company *Sandia National Laboratory* tested EyeDentify Inc. on several hundred volunteers. The result was a zero false accept rate and false reject rate less than 1% [27]. However, at that time, the testing of biometric systems was in its early stages, so we cannot be sure of the objectivity of the test.

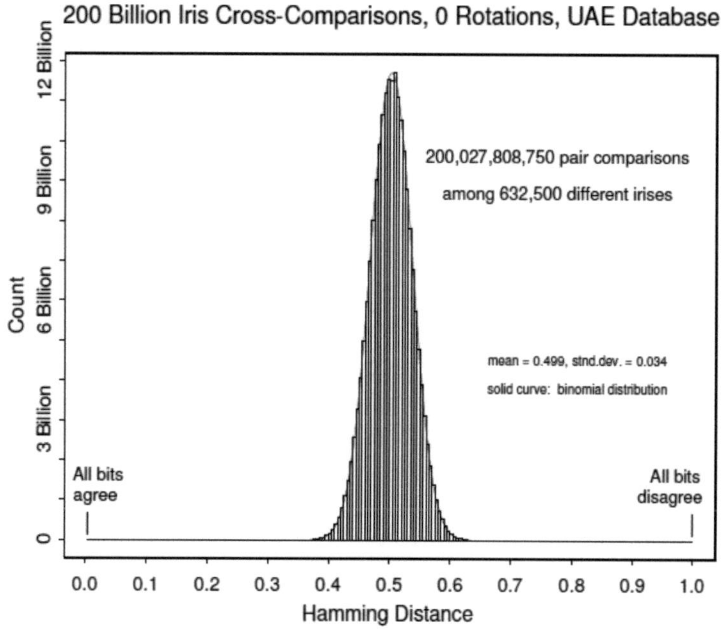

Figure 21. Hamming distance distribution [26].

According to EyeDentify, the frequency distribution of the image of each eye compared to any other one approached a very ideal Gaussian curve with a mean value of 0.144 and a standard deviation of 0.176. The corresponding probability of this distribution with a given mean value and a standard deviation of 0.7 is about one million [26].

The retinal identification method is prone to some conditions that need to be met during scanning. Conditions that might raise the false reject rate are, for example, incorrect distance between sensor and eye, dirty optics, contact lens edges, and glasses. Also, ambient lighting results in the subconscious narrowing of the pupil, so sometimes the device cannot be operated well in outdoor conditions during daylight hours.

4.3. Anti-spoofing

4.3.1. Iris

There are several possibilities on how to test the liveness (anti-spoofing) of the iris. The most common is the iris reaction to a change in light when the pupil diminishes with more intense lighting. This reflex is subconscious, and responses are usually within the range of 250–400 ms. The pupil stretches and expands even under a constant illumination, and this periodic phenomenon is called the *hippus* [28].

Another way of anti-spoofing can be eye movement, or blinking by the command of a scanning device.

Spectrographic properties of tissues, fats, and blood are used by more advanced devices. Blood reflects infrared radiation very well, as well as the iris pigment melanin. This phenomenon is called the *coaxial back retina reflection*, also called "red eyes," when the light is reflected from a pink retina back into the camera.

Purkyne's reflection from the surface of the cornea and the lens can also be used to test the liveness of the eye. When a suitable light source illuminates the surface of the eye, reflective images are produced that are reflected from the front and back surfaces of the cornea and the lens.

4.3.2. Retina

Retinal scanning of the eye is a relatively problematic process that cannot be easily imitated. To cheat such a sensor, it would be necessary to use a spoofed eye with the same characteristics as a live eye, which is a very complicated and nearly impossible to replicate (the use of medical ophthalmologic eye phantoms should be taken into account). There is not much information about the liveness test on the retina, but it could again take advantage of medical information, for example, that the non-living retina has a different color. Light refraction of the retina or blood flow in blood vessels may also be tested.

Since the eye is a very sensitive organ, an invasive method cannot be used for this reason. There is a similar liveness test as for the iris; however, this testing can be used to cheat the system when the right eye is replaced by a false (spoofed) eye after a successful test life. For this reason, it is more appropriate to test liveness with another method. The first test is to test the color of the yellow spot. It is done during the use of the scanned eye. It is only with the dead person that the yellow spot becomes yellow, until then it is reddish.

Another option is to test liveness using eye movements. The same principle is used in medicine when examining the eye background. The medical doctor needs to see the whole retina and not just the part seen from a direct view. Therefore, the device is equipped with a deliberate point that the patient watches to slightly retract the eye, allowing the doctor to monitor almost the entire retina. This principle can also be used to test for liveness. The device is equipped with a similar observation point and moves it several times. In each relocation, it performs scans of the retina and compares the position of the blind or the yellow spot. If it is in another place after each scan, it is a living eye.

4.4. Related standards

4.4.1. Iris

- *ANSI INCITS 379–2004: Information Technology: Iris Image Interchange Format* [29]. Describes the format for exchanging iris image information. This includes the definition of attributes, data and sample logging, and compliance criteria.
- *ISO/IEC 19794–6: 2011: Information Technology—Biometric Data Interchange Formats—Part 6: Iris Image Data* [29, 30]. Specifies two alternative formats for data representation. The first one is based on direct storage in an uncompressed format, the other requires some preprocessing; however, the data are compact and only carry the iris information.

4.4.2. Retina

There are no biometric standards available for recognizing the retina; however, basically, these are images of the bloodstream as well as hand vein recognition, that is, comparable standards could be taken into account. Just only medical standards for retina scanning are available, for example, ISO 10943:2011—Ophthalmic Instruments—Indirect Ophthalmoscopes or ISO/TR 20824:2007—Ophthalmic Instruments—Background for Light Hazard Specification in Ophthalmic Instrument Standards.

4.5. Commercial applications and devices

4.5.1. Iris

There are many examples of practical applications. The most common systems are in the United Arab Emirates, where they are located in airports and seaports (about 3.8 million comparisons daily). Another example is the system at Schiphol Airport in the Netherlands, which is used by people with high-frequency flights. Another example is an application in Tokyo. Condominium employees use this system to enter, while at the same time a lift is called to take them to their office. In Afghanistan, the UNHC (*United Nations High Commission*) uses iris recognition to control immigrants from neighboring countries.

Available devices capable of human iris identification also exist in a relatively large amount. **Figure 22** shows the *Panasonic BM-ET200, EyeLock Nano,* and *Iritech* scanners. Other manufacturers are *Iris ID Systems* and *iCAM TD100, IrisGuard Inc., Iritech Inc., AOptix Technologies,* among several others.

4.5.2. Retina

The use of retinal recognition is appropriate in areas with high security requirements such as nuclear development, arms development, as well as manufacturing, government and military bases, secret organizations, and so on.

Figure 22. Panasonic BM-ET200; EyeLock Nano; Iritech.

A pioneer in developing these identification systems is primarily EyeDentify, which designed and manufactured the EyeDentify 7.5 EyeDentificationSystem (see **Figure 23**) and its latest ICAM 2001 model, which was designed in 2001.

Others are *Retinal Technologies*, known since 2004 as Retica Systems, but details of their system are not known.

The company *TPI* (Trans Pacific Int.) has recently offered an ICAM 2001-like sensor, but there is no longer any information available.

At the end of this subchapter, we devote our attention to our own construction of an interesting and nonexistent device that can be used both in the field of biometric systems and in the field of ophthalmology. This device is a fully automatic non-mydriatic fundus camera. Many years ago, we started with a simple device (see **Figure 24** on the left), but over time, we came to the third generation of the device (see **Figure 24** on the right). We are now working on the fourth generation of this device that will be fully automatic. The original concept was focused only on the retina (a direct view in the optical axis of the eye), then we arrived (second generation) to retrieve the retina and the iris of the eye in one device, while the third and fourth generations are again focused only on the retina of the eye. The

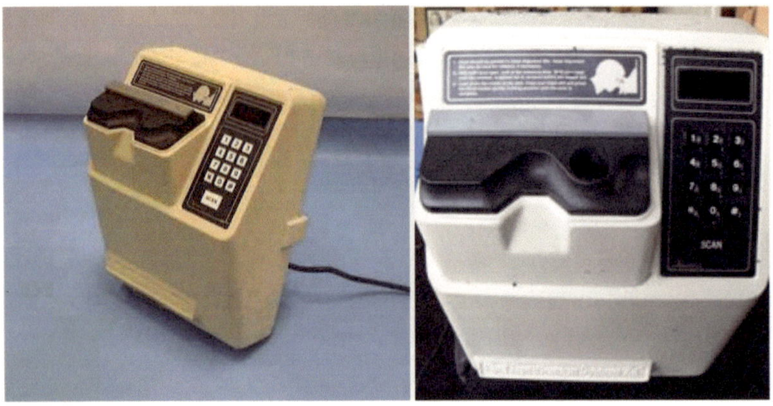

Figure 23. EyeDentify 7.5 EyeDentificationSystem [31].

Figure 24. A non-mydriatic fundus camera of our own development—first generation on the left, second generation in the middle, and third generation on the right.

http://dx.doi.org/10.5772/intechopen.76026

third generation can already find the eye in the camera, move the optical system to the center of the image (alignment of the optical axis of the eye and the camera), and take pictures of the eye retina (in visible spectrum) to shoot a short video (in infrared spectrum). The fourth generation will be able to capture almost the entire ocular background (not just a direct view in the optical axis of the eye) and combine the image into one file. This will, certainly, be associated with software that can already find the macula and blind spot, arteries, vessels, detect and extract bifurcations and crossings, and find areas with potential pathological findings, while we can detect exudates/druses and hemorrhages, including the calculation of their area. In the future, we focus on the reliability and accuracy of detectors and extractors, including other types of illnesses that will be in the main interests of ophthalmologists.

5. Conclusion

This chapter describes biometric identification based on the internal organs of the eye, retina, and iris. These methods are very accurate and used in areas with the highest safety requirements. The features to identify the eye are very unique in each individual, and the likelihood of finding two of the exact same identifiers is much smaller than, for example, a fingerprint.

While iris recognition devices are relatively well known just for their seamlessness and relatively good user-friendliness, it is not so for the retina. Currently, there is no device for eye retina recognition. All the devices sold so far have not been successful mainly because of their relatively poor user-friendly interface. This method is used more where there is a high demand toward the deception of the sensors; a relatively complicated retinal scanning process guarantees a certain degree of safety against the replication of a retinal specimen.

Acknowledgements

This work was supported by The Ministry of Education, Youth and Sports of the Czech Republic from the National Programme of Sustainability (NPU II); project *IT4Innovations excellence in science—LQ1602*.

Author details

Martin Drahanský

Address all correspondence to: drahan@fit.vutbr.cz

Faculty of Information Technology, Centre of Excellence IT4Innovations, Brno University of Technology, Brno, Czech Republic

References

[1] Daugman J. Biometric Personal Identification System Based on Iris Analysis. U.S. Patent No. 5,291,560 issued on 1994-03-01

[2] Available from: http://www.jouefct.com/great-sample-detail-human-eye-anatomy-gallery/

[3] Available from: https://onewandering.wordpress.com/2009/04/15/windows-or-crypts-to-my-super-fabulous-soul/

[4] Kronfeld P. Gross anatomy and embryology of the eye. In: Davson H, editor. The Eye – Vol. 1 Vegetative Physiology and Biochemistry. New York: Academic Press; 1962

[5] Roberts JE. Update on the positive effects of light in humans. Photochemistry and Photobiology. 2005;**81**:490-492. DOI: 10.1562/2004-12-02-IR-391.1

[6] Daugman J. How Iris recognition works. IEEE Transactions on Circuits and Systems for Video Technology. 2004;**14**(1):21-30

[7] Lee K, Byeon O, Kim T, Lim S. Efficient Iris recognition through improvement of feature vector and classifier. ETRI Journal. 2001;**23**(2):61-70

[8] Noh S, Kim J, Bae K. Iris Feature Extraction Using Independent Component Analysis. AVBPA. Springer; 2003

[9] Tan T, Wang Y, Zhang D, Ma L. Efficient Iris recognition by characterizing key local variations. IEEE Transactions on Image Processing. 2004;**13**(6):739-750

[10] Berggren L. Iridology. Acta Ophthalmologica. 1985;**63**(1):8. DOI: 10.1111/j.1755-3768.1985.tb05205.x

[11] Rods and Cones of the Human Eye. https://askabiologist.asu.edu/rods-and-cones [Accessed on January 02, 2018]

[12] Albert DM, Miller JW, et al. Principles and Practice of Ophthalmology. 3rd ed2008. ISBN: 978-1-4160-0016-7

[13] Ryan SJ. Retina. Elsevier Mosby; 2006. ISBN: 0323043232

[14] Lékaři. Online: http://www.lekari-online.cz/ocni-lekarstvi/novinky/degenerace-zlute-skvrny [Accessed on December 23, 2017]

[15] Scanlon PH, Wilkinson CP, Aldington SJ, Matthews DR. A Practical Manual of Diabetic Retinopathy Management. Wiley-Blackwell; 2009. ISBN: 978-1-405-17035-2

[16] Říhová E. Uveitidy. Grada Publishing; 2009. ISBN: 978-80-247-2897-1

[17] Timberlake GT, Kennedy M. The Direct Ophthalmoscope – How it Works and How to Use it. University of Kansas; 2005. p. 39. Available online on: http://web.media.mit.edu/~raskar/Eye/TheDirectOphthalmoscope.pdf

[18] Goldstein I, Simon C. A New Scientific Method of Identification. New York State Journal of Medicine. 1935;**35**:901-906

[19] Tower P. The fundus oculi in monozygotic twins: Report of six pairs of identical twins. AMA Arch Ophthalmology. 1955;**54**:225-239

[20] Hill RB. Retina Identification. In: Biometrics: Personal Identification in Networked Society. New York: Springer; 1996. pp. 123-141

[21] Optimis Fusion: http://www.askin.cz/prednesegmentove/ [Accessed on December 05, 2017]

[22] Kowa VX-20: http://dfv.com.au/products/diagnostic/diagnostic-imaging/kowa-vx-20-mydriatic-non-mydriatic-integrated-fundus-camera/ [Accessed on December 05, 2017]

[23] Hill RB. U.S. Patent 4,620,318; 1986. http://www.freepatentsonline.com/4620318.pdf

[24] Arndt JH. U.S. Patent 4,923,297; 1990. http://www.freepatentsonline.com/4923297.pdf

[25] Johnson JC, Hill RB. U.S. Patent 5,532,771. http://www.freepatentsonline.com/5532771.pdf

[26] Daugman J. John Daugman's Webpage. Cambridge University. http://www.cl.cam.ac.uk/~jgd1000/UAEsummary.pdf [Accessed on December 23, 2017]

[27] Holmes JP, Wright LJ, Maxwell RL. A Performance Evaluation of Biometric Identification Devices. USA: Sandia National Laboratories; 1991. Technical Report SAND91-0276

[28] Bouma H, Baghuis LCJ. Hippus of the pupil: Periods of slow oscillations of unknown origin. Vision Research. 1971;**11**(11):1345-1351

[29] Tabassi E. Iris *Quality* Standardization. NIST, Iris Exchange; 2014. Available online: https://www.nist.gov/sites/default/files/documents/2016/12/05/xx_thursday_tabassi_iris_q_std.pdf

[30] ISO/IEC 19794-6: 2011. Information Technology – Biometric Data Interchange Formats – Part 6: Iris Image Data. https://www.iso.org/standard/50868.html

[31] https://cryptologicfoundation.org/visit/museum/acquisitions/acquisitionarchivessection/individualequipmentitems/rfsignalgenerator.html [Accessed on January 03, 2018]

Chapter 3

A Survey on Soft Biometrics for Human Identification

Abdelgader Abdelwhab and Serestina Viriri

Additional information is available at the end of the chapter

http://dx.doi.org/10.5772/intechopen.76021

Abstract

The focus has been changed to multi-biometrics due to the security demands. The ancillary information extracted from primary biometric (face and body) traits such as facial measurements, gender, color of the skin, ethnicity, and height is called soft biometrics and can be integrated to improve the speed and overall system performance of a primary biometric system (e.g., fuse face with facial marks) or to generate human semantic interpretation description (qualitative) of a person and limit the search in the whole dataset when using gender and ethnicity (e.g., old African male with blue eyes) in a fusion framework. This chapter provides a holistic survey on soft biometrics that show major works while focusing on facial soft biometrics and discusses some of the features of extraction and classification techniques that have been proposed and show their strengths and limitations.

Keywords: multi-biometrics, primary biometric, soft biometrics, gender, facial, ethnicity, fusion methods

1. Introduction

Along with the automation of our modem life, security issues become more critical and important. There are questions asked in our daily life such as "is this the right person to be allowed to access the system?", "is this the authorized person to perform such action?", and "does this person belong to this country?" [1]. There were two methods for answering this questions: first one based on "what you have" and called (knowledge factors), such as ID cards, and the second one based on "what you know" and called (ownership factors), such as passwords as shown in **Figure 1**. However both methods can be borrowed or copied or stolen, so users need to carry many IDs and memorize a lot of passwords. As reported banks, telecommunication companies, and governments are losing millions of dollars annually because of the violations of their password-based and card-based security police [2]. To solve this person identification issue, biometrics is an opened field.

Figure 1. Information sets.

Biometrics rely on *what you are* called (inherence factors) so can natively differentiate between a permitted and illegal person [3, 4]. Biometric traits offer the following advantages [5]:

- They are unique for each individual.
- They cannot easily be forgotten, stolen, borrowed, shared, or observed.
- They always vary and are always available.
- They cannot easily be transferred to another individual.

A biometric-based security system is almost impossible to be fooled. The word biometric is a composite word bios, which refers to life, and metron, which refers to measure, coming from the Greek language. Biometric is sometimes defined as a research area focused on measuring and analyzing a person's unique characteristics [6] to identify or verify a person identity and is an essential daily task for a security system to make sure that the services are available for the permitted users only [7]. It can be divided into traditional, primary, and soft biometrics as shown: traditional biometric deals with physical, behavioral, and biological characteristics such as facial features, eye, signature, gait, voice, DNA, and fingerprints as shown in **Figure 2**. Soft biometrics are concerned with ancillary characteristics that provide some information not enough to identify a person clearly as gender, ethnicity, skin color, scars, and height [8, 9]. Behavioral or physiological human features must fulfill the following requirements to be recognized as can be used as a biometric characteristic [7, 10]:

1. Universal: each person has the trait.
2. Acceptable: available when needed.
3. Resistance to circumvention: not easy to cheat.
4. Distinctive: can be used to differentiate between persons.
5. Permanence: they don't change over a period of time.
6. Collectable: the characteristic can be easily collected and measured.

http://dx.doi.org/10.5772/intechopen.76021

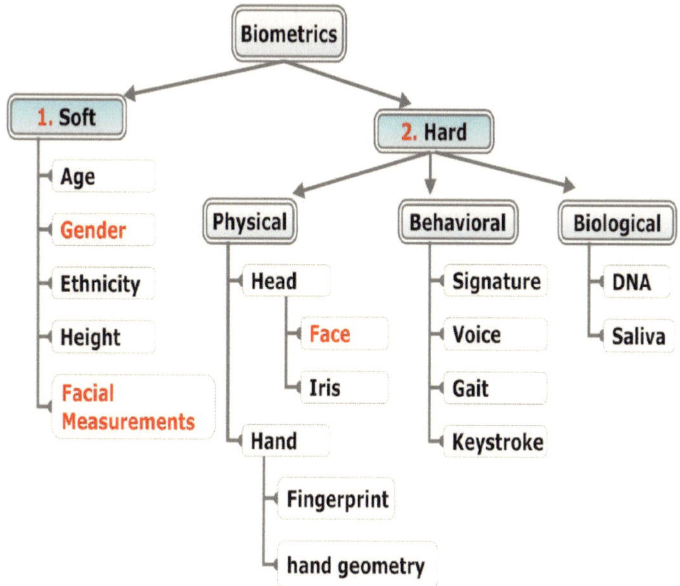

Figure 2. Biometrics type.

However, there is not a single biometric feature that satisfies all these characteristics identified above yet, so as a result, none of existing biometric system provides a precise foolproof recognition, so there is a gap for improving the recognition accuracy and speed of primary biometrics using soft biometrics.

This chapter is divided into five sections as follows: Section 2 shows the soft biometric benefits, unimodal biometric system limitation and how multimodal biometric system overcome this limitation, the need of biometric fusion for system performance, and the system performance measurement. A holistic survey on related works is presented in Section 3 while focusing on facial soft biometrics. In Section 4 we show the challenges and the limitations of the soft biometrics. Section 5 concludes the work.

2. Soft biometrics

Soft biometrics provide ancillary information but are not fully distinctive and permanent, so these features cannot provide a reliable person recognition. However, such ancillary information still can be used as a secondary information to complement the primary biometric traits (face, iris, etc.), and these features can be classified to physique (e.g., color skin, gender, ethnic origin), clothing (e.g., clothes' color), or accessories (e.g., glasses, hat) [11].

2.1. Benefits of soft biometrics

- Can be used to improve the recognition accuracy and speed of a primary biometric system [12].

- Can be used when there is a difficulty to collect a primary biometric trait or the collected data is not clear due to the sensor error or data collected from a distance with no cooperation with the user.
- Acceptable: collecting data for identification don't need cooperation between the person and the sensor and available.
- Soft facial biometrics are not expensive to compute since they can be acquired at the same time during primary face biometric collection.
- Enrolling person needs no cooperation and taken at distance even training of the system is done offline.
- Soft biometric bridges the gap between machine and human since they have a semantic meaning and can be understood by the human as old and short African male.
- Soft biometrics don't rise a privacy concern about collecting and saving data because they provide ancillary description and are not fully distinctive as old and short male.
- Filtering and indexing the large database to limit the number of searched data according to the connected person characteristics [13], for example, we can restrict the search for female gender.

2.2. Biometric system

It is an essential pattern recognition system that uses the human characteristics in order to identify the person divided into unimodal system when using single trait and one that uses more than single traits called multi-biometric [14]; when developing a reliable biometric system, there are some concerns that need to be analyzed and balanced as needed [7]:

- Harmless to the users, as reported a research company put a SIM card under the skin for authentication.
- Performance, which means the highest recognition rate and system speed, while tolerance the environmental factors affecting the system, stable and time invariant.
- Acceptability, are the people ready to use their biometric trait?
- Circumvention means how easily your system can be overcome or bypassed using fake techniques.
- Accessible, easy to use.

Unimodal systems suffer from low-resolution data due to the person or the sensor, and this can lead to high failure to enroll rate, lacking people coverage area, and low recognition rate because cooperation with the user is needed to collect the data. So it is almost difficult to get very high recognition rates using unimodal system [14]; to improve the recognition rate, we need to acquire more than one trait from the same sensor or multiple sensors, but while increasing the recognition rate, the complexity and processing, which is time-consuming, increase.

Some problems associated with the unimodal biometric systems can be overcome by the use of the multi-biometric systems that combine the information obtained from multiple sources [15]. Still, such a system has two major limitations: first, the overall cost to construct the system can be prohibitive due to the need for more high-quality sensors, large storage capacity, and computational requirements. Second, the system requires a longer time for verification, hence causing inconvenience to the users [10]. However, soft biometrics are the solution to decrease the cost by using the same sensor [10]. The main steps for a biometric system are as follow [7, 16] as shown in **Figure 3**:

- Enrollment is the first step where biometric traits of the person are collected by the sensor and saved to the dataset as a template for verification purpose and later on used for identification. Successful biometric enrollment is necessary for the next steps.
- Enhancing the stored data to get high recognition rate by doing preprocessing as histogram equalization, clipping the area of interest dealing with the illumination.
- Extracting features vector from the individual for identification and match it with the stored template data.
- Template dataset: enrolling data means storing biometric data to the dataset as a template to be compared with the stored one. In the case of authentication, biometric data are matched against a reference template from the template database.
- Classification and matching: biometric feature data are validated against the template data in the dataset
- Decision can be rejected or accepted according to the matching similarity score or the threshold value.

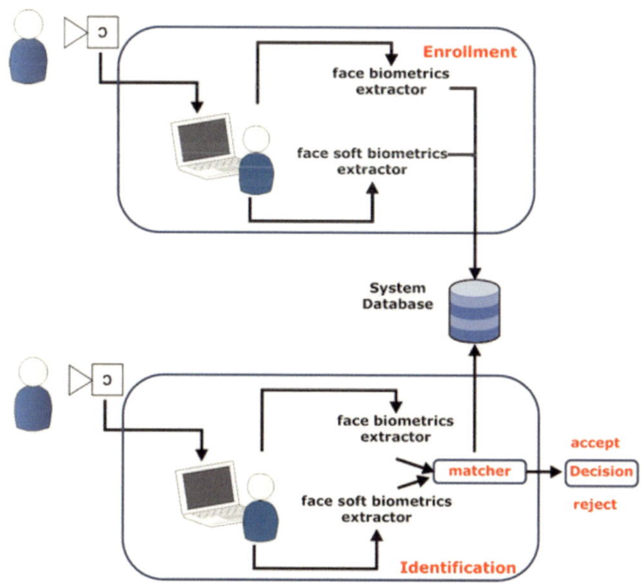

Figure 3. Biometric system enrollment and identification diagram.

Biometric system can work in two modes:

Identification either in identification mode or verification mode. Identification mode works as one to many by comparing the individual with all the templates stored in the dataset, while a verification mode works as one to one by comparing the individual with his own template stored in the dataset.

2.3. Biometric fusion

Biometric data may change over time or affected by environmental condition, so by fusing more than one trait or same trait from more than one source, we overcome the unimodal limitation and try to reduce one or more of the rejection and acceptance error rate based on the system requirements [17] as shown in **Figure 4**. Moreover, there is no one best biometrics since different applications require different policies such as distance learning, border control, and national identity card that require low false accept rate and failure to enroll. However, fusion is key to increase the recognition rate and can be taken at different stages (sensor, decision, feature extraction, classification stage).

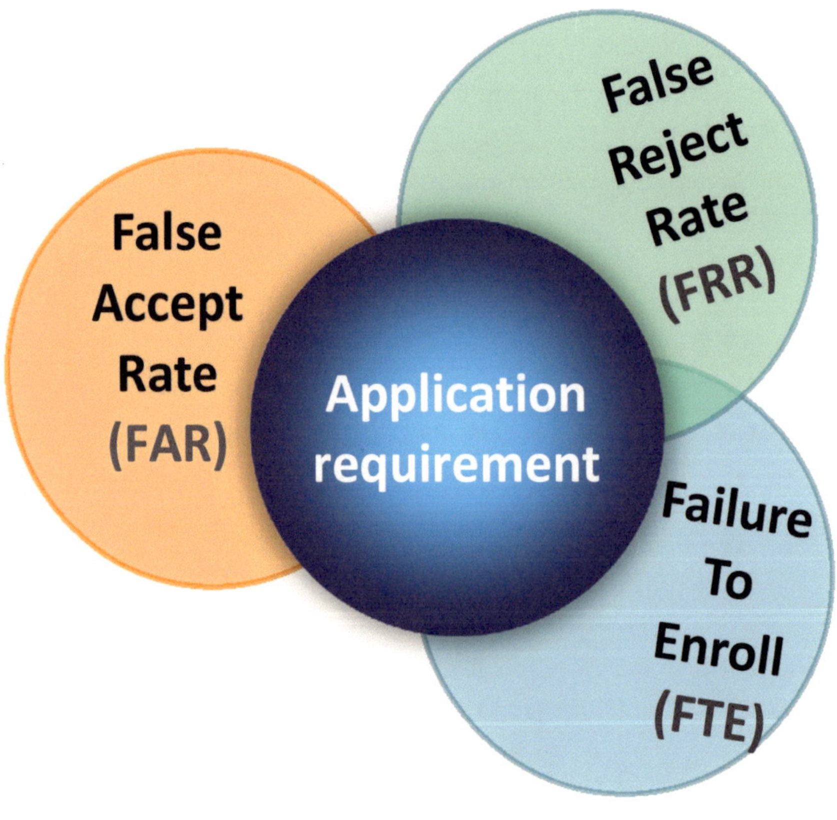

Figure 4. Performance evaluation.

Sanderson and Paliwal et al. [18] divide the fusion into two categories: before classification called pre-matching and after classification called post-matching as shown in **Figure 5**:

- Pre-classification fusion [19–21]: before the classification level, the integration can be done in two ways as followed:

  1. Sensor level: integrating the raw data is difficult because it has a lot of unimportant features not only the region of interest and data collected from the sensors can be suffered from noisy as nonuniform illumination. Sensor-level fusion refers to raw data obtained using multiple sensors or multiple snapshots of a biometric using a single sensor. Face images collected from multiple sources with different resolutions may not be possible to integrate together.
  2. Feature level: in feature-level fusion, we get a lot of information by producing one feature set from fusing different features that are extracted from the captured images. So feature sets need to be tuned, normalized, transformed, and reduced. In practice, it is difficult to achieve feature-level fusion because concatenating different features may lead to dimensionality problem.

- Post-classification fusion [19–22]: the integration after the classification can be divided into three types:

  1. At score stage [23]: scores combined to generate one score value to and used for making decision according to the threshold value. Threshold making the system more reliable than using true and false since there is range can be tuned to increase or decrease the false acceptance rate and false rejected rate. However, a lower threshold decreases the rate of falsely rejected rate but also increases the rate of falsely accepted rate.

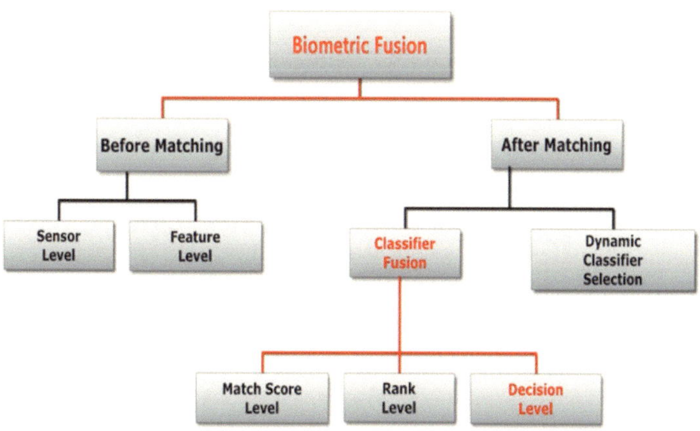

Figure 5. Fusion levels.

2. At rank stage [24]: the score values are arranged in descending order showing the possibility of the decision that at top list most preferred classes are placed and at down list least preferred classes.

3. Decision stage depends totally on the result value of the score stage, and final decision is taken whether the identified person is fake to reject or a unique to accept. Each classifier provides a hard decision. The decisions can be combined using:

- Majority voting:
- Decision is taken when a majority of the classifiers declare the same decision. To ensure a decision is taken, we must have classifiers more than the number of classes.
- Logic operator (and, or):
- And operator means all the classifiers give the same result whether reject or accept, and it is good when low false acceptance is required. Or operator is useful when low false reject is required.
- Fuzzy logic [25]:
- Instead of having reject or accept, we have a truth value between two values.

2.4. Performance evaluation

A biometric system needs to be evaluated and tested; there are some measurement concepts for evaluation as equal, false rejection and false acceptance rate [1, 26]:

- EER means both rate false accept and false reject are equal, and the more the EER, the more accurate the system is. The FRR refers to the rate of permitted users but are rejected by the system falsely.
- FAR means how many people don't have permission but the system accepts them as authorized person and falsely accepted.
- Failure to enroll (FTE) concerned with the rate of individuals not able to enroll in the system.
- FRR: the number of the authorized person but falsely rejected by the system.
- Failure to capture (FTC) concerned with the biometric traits are presented correctly, but the system was not able to capture them correctly.

$$\text{FRR} = (\text{number of false rejected}/\text{NAA}) \times 100\% \tag{1}$$

$$\text{FAR} = (\text{number of false accepted}/\text{NIA}) \times 100\% \tag{2}$$

NIA means number of impostor attempts and NAA means number of authorized attempts. The accuracy and recognition rate and performance measurements of a biometric system can be affected by some factors [26]:

- Environmental factors as high temperature, steam, and rain humidity lead to low accuracy. The features change over time as age and performance. The age, gender, ethnic, and face pose.
- User willing and wishes: since users don't need to deal with the system intentionally, the system get affected and accuracy decrease.
- The plastic surgery patients and people who don't have a hand cannot use a fingerprint.

  All the measurement rates are affected by the above factors, so any biometric system needs to calculate the error factors and tune and normalize them according to the system requirements and nature.

3. Literature review and related work

Alphonse Bertillon, who firstly introduced the idea of personal identification system based on biometric, morphological, and anthropometric using color of the eyes, hair, and skin in 1896. Face recognition is lower in uniqueness and more acceptable than iris but still is user-friendly, and people are willing to use it than other techniques [27]. The soft biometric is divided into three groups as follows [28]:

- Global traits are used for dataset indexing that remain fixed for the whole life as ethnicity and sex.
- Body features are used to describe an individual height and weight as tall or fat.
- Head features, this is where the research is heading now because of the rich feature in this body part as facial measurements and skin and hair color.

Soft biometric traits also can be classified according to permanence and distinctiveness as shown in **Table 1**. The permanence of a trait shows the strength of the trait over the period of time as gender and ethnicity don't change over time. Distinctiveness refers to the ability of a trait to differentiate between individuals.

Soft biometric traits	Face	Permanence	Distinctiveness
Facial measurements	Face	High	Medium
Gender	Face	High	Low
Skin color	Face	Medium	Low
Eye color	Face	Medium	Medium
Tattoo	Face	High	High
Age	Face	Low	Medium
Mustache	Face	Low	Low

Table 1. Facial soft biometric traits.

In this paper, we are focusing on the head soft biometric features. As shown in **Table 2**, humans can easily be identified by their faces because they don't change over a period of time and widely. According to Lin [47], face features provide different information when resized or clipped or shown from different sides.

The related works show some of the major works presented in timeline order starting from 2000 up to 2017 as shown in **Table 2**.

Jain and Dass et al. [13] the father of soft biometric who introduced it as ancillary information, but are not able to individually authenticate the person due to the lake of distinctiveness and permanence. They propose to use demographic information (gender, ethnicity, and height) as soft biometrics to improve the primary fingerprint system. Experiments show that recognition performance of fingerprint increased 5% by using soft biometrics.

Pedro and Julian et al. [28] experimental result shows that soft biometrics can be used as a secondary information to improve the primary biometrics and they can be acquired from distance; fusion is taken at score stage. Park and Jain et al. [34] use three feature extraction techniques:

- Active appearance model for extracting facial features as nose and eyes
- Laplacian of Gaussian
- Morphological operators

Two datasets are used to evaluate the system. They show that the use of soft biometrics (ethnicity, gender, facial marks) increases the recognition rate. Soft biometric traits can be considered as an alternative when face images are occluded or partially damaged. Gender and ethnicity of a person do not change over the lifetime, so they can be used to purge the database to narrow the search list. However, performance increased, but complexity also increased, and facial mark extraction depends on the image resolution and controlled environment needed.

Dantcheva and Velardo et al. [48] introduce two new soft biometric traits, called body weight and clothes color. Related promising results on the performance are provided. Dantcheva and Dugelay et al. [35] use eyes, skin, and hair color traits and cascade classifier; performance increased and balanced between complexity and performance. However, system suffers from illumination and poses, evaluated under one dataset and controlled environment. Soft biometric traits collected from a distance without user cooperation as shown by Denman and Fookes et al. [31] propose head and body traits and system evaluated using PETS 2006 small dataset and recognition rate decreased but the system can be used when primary data not available. Niinuma and Jain et al. [33] propose framework for continuous user authentication that uses clothing and skin colors fused with password. Soft biometric traits collected automatically every time user login with his password. Experiment results show the method effectiveness for continuous user authentication. However, system is evaluated with one dataset and suffering from illumination.

Ref.	Modalities	Database	Techniques	Results
[16] 2000	• Face • Voice • Lip movement	• 150 persons for 3 months • A sample of audio and video frames	• Optical-flow technique • Fourier transformation • Hausdorff face location measurement • Synergetic	• Performance increased, and the false acceptance rate decreased
[10] 2004	• Fingerprint • Gender • Ethnicity • Height	160 subjects	Bayes rule	The recognition rate increased by 6%
[29] 2008	Tattoo(human, plant, flag, symbol, object)	• Image Database Web-based tattoo • Michigan State Police Tattoo Database (MI-DB)	• Scale-invariant feature transformer (SIFT) • Difference of Gaussian • Local extrema detection • Key point matching	Performance increased to 77.2% on (MI-DB) and 98.6% on (web-based tattoo)
[30] 2008	• Height • Body size • Gender • Stride/step	• USF outdoor dataset • SET HD indoor dataset	A novel gait analysis in video surveillance	Height, gender, and body size show a better performance over stride/step lengths
[31] 2009	• Legs, head color and size	PETS 2006	Active appearance model	The error rate is decreased
[11] 2009	• Face • Facial marks	• FERET • Mugshot	• Morphological Operators • AAM • Laplacian of Gaussian	System performance increased by 3 percentage to become 94.14%

Ref.	Modalities	Database	Techniques	Results
[32] 2009	• Height and color of: ○ Head ○ Torso ○ Legs	Subset of the PETS 2006	—	Equal error rate of 6.1% is achieved
[33] 2010	• Face • Face color • Body location and size • Cloth color	Video frames for 20 persons	• PCA (Eigen) • Haar classifier • Bhattacharyya coefficient	• Real-time identification • Not affected by the person position
[34] 2010	• Face • Gender • Ethnicity • Facial marks (scars, moles, freckles)	• FERET • Mugshot	• AAM • Gaussian • PCA • Morphological operators	• The fusion of soft biometrics is able to improve the performance of face recognition • Facial marks can help in discriminating identical twins
[35] 2010	• Skin color • Hair color • Eye color • Beard • Mustache • Glasses	Color FERET with 646 people	• AdaBoost • Cascade • Histogram-based Bayes	• A proper balance between complexity and performance • Increase system reliability
[36] 2011	• Facial measurement of the lips and eyes • Face	Yale	• Biohashing • Hamming distances • Absolute differences	The error rates have been decreased

Ref.	Modalities	Database	Techniques	Results
[37] 2011	• Sunglasses • Scarf	AR Face	• Gabor wavelets • PCA • SVM	Recognition rate has increased
[38] 2012	Anthropometric body measures	• Medical chimera dataset • NHANES dataset • FERET dataset	Eigenfaces	Anthropometric features improve performance in both accuracy and recognition speed
[39] 2012	• Gender • Height • Weight • Blood group	• IMS-BHU Indian hospital	• Principal component analysis (PCA) • Independent component analysis (ICA) • Linear discriminant analysis (LDA) [27] • Local binary pattern (LBP) • Speeded up robust features (SURF)	Soft biometrics improve primary face biometric performance by 6.5%
[40] 2013	• Facial measurement • Skin color • Hair color	Face94	• Wavelet characterization • SVM	The recognition rate increased, equal error rate decreased, and skin color highly increases the performance
[41] 2013	Facial wrinkles	Well-known people from the Internet with high resolution	• Bipartite graph matching algorithm • Curves to Line segments algorithm • Modified Hausdorff distance (MHD) • Curve proximity distance (CPD)	• 88% achieved by MHD • 87 achieved by CPD • CPD performs better than MHD • Fusing MHD and CPD increases the recognition rate to 93%

Ref.	Modalities	Database	Techniques	Results
[42] 2014	• Eyebrow size • Eye-to-eyebrow distance • Eyebrow length	Southampton with video recordings from more than 200 subjects	Viola-Jones	The performance increased to 100% when using ten persons only
[43] 2014	• Clothing attribute (head, upper body, lower body, foot, attached to body)	• Soton Gait database	• Soft-margin ranking SVM • Formulation of similarity constraints	The identification rate increased from 78% to 95%
[44] 2015	Clothe color and type	Online shopping-labeled dataset	• Deep learning based • RCNN detector • SV regression	The performance increased but more dataset for training the module needed
[45] 2015	Body parts (clothe, hair, color)	VIPeR and GRID dataset	Multilevel CNN	Classification rate increased by 9% than support vector machine
[46] 2017	• Eyebrow length • Eye size • Noise width	Labeled faces in the wild Dataset	• GIST descriptor • Deformable part model	Accuracy rate increased using comparative features

Table 2. List of some of these works.

Asma and Souhir et al. [40] use facial measurements and skin and hair color as soft biometric traits. Support vector machine as a classifier is evaluated using one dataset. Results show equal error rate is decreased and recognition rate improved and requires no more cost since soft biometric traits are collected at the time of primary biometric collection by the same sensor. However, system needs to be tested with more difficult dataset and compared with another system. On the other hand, facial measurement features are very sensitive to pose and expression variation.

Nawaf and Nixon et al. [42] consider the eyebrow measurement distance and length from crowd sourcing. System is evaluated under one dataset with one classifier. Recognition rate increases but still needs to be tested with another dataset and compared with different classifiers. Jain and Park et al. [11] fuse face and facial marks. Their results show system performance increased up to 94.14%, but still facial mark extraction depends on the image resolution.

Min and Hadid et al. [37] propose facial occlusions as sunglasses, scarf, eye color, beard mustache, and glasses' traits. Experimental result shows that facial occlusions affect the system performance especially when user tries to use it to prevent himself from being recognized. However, they used one dataset for evaluation and did not compare it with other systems. Chen and Huang et al. [44] define new soft biometric traits to describe people based on their clothes' type, color, and pattern. RCNN body detector is used. However, they used their own dataset taken under controlled environment for training the RCNN, so the system cannot be compared with different systems and neural network needs more training data.

Jain, Dass, and Nandakumar et al. [10] combine gender, height, and ethnicity as soft biometric traits with fingerprint. The system performance increased by 6%. However, soft biometric traits did not extract automatically, and the system is evaluated by 160 subjects only. Lee, Jain, and Jin et al. [29] achieve a recognition rate of 98.6% on Web-DB with good quality taken under controlled environment and 77.2% on Michigan State Police Tattoo Database (MI-DB) using scale-invariant feature transform (SIFT) feature extractor. Experiment results show scars, marks, and tattoos (SMT) are more distinctive than other demographic biometrics such as ethnicity, gender, and weight to identify a person. However, tattoo dataset is collected under controlled environment at booking time.

Batool, Nazre, and Sima et al. [41] report a classification accuracy of 88% for facial wrinkles as a soft biometrics using modified Hausdorff distance (MHD) algorithm. There is no standard dataset to evaluate the system and compare with the other one. However, wrinkles are extracted manually by hand, and detecting wrinkles needs high-resolution image. Velardo, Carmelo, and Jean-Luc et al. [38] present a human body measurement (anthropometry) to prune primary biometric dataset. Their own medical dataset is collected from Indian hospital used for evaluating the body measurements and FERET data for face recognition. Results show system accuracy and recognition speed increased.

Saini and Sinha et al. [36] integrate the face and facial measurement of the lips and eyes as distance between two pupils, distance between the eyes and the lips, and length of the lips and the eyes to improve the recognition rate using hamming, absolute difference, and biohashing distance techniques. Experiment results on Yale dataset show error rate is decreased. However biohashing performances are poor when the tokenized random numbers are compromised; also only one dataset is used and results are not compared with another system.

Tiwari S, Singh A, and Singh SK et al. [39] propose an optimal framework for newborn recognition by fusing match scores from face and soft biometrics. Results on IMS-BHU Indian hospital dataset show that soft biometrics improve recognition rate by 5.6% over the primary biometric. However framework evaluated on one dataset has high-resolution image taken under controlled pose and illumination.

Jaha, Emad, and Mark et al. [43] show clothing traits can be used for identification of individual where clothing descriptions might be the only available feature. An, Chen, Kafai, Yang, and Bhanu et al. [49] aim to improve the re-identification performance by re-ranking the returned results based on soft biometric attributes. Experiments on challenging benchmark VIPeR dataset show that reranking improves the recognition accuracy.

4. Challenges and future work

Multimodal biometric systems are used to overcome the unimodal biometric system limitations by collecting multiple traits from multiple sensors. However, such a system will decrease the performance by increasing the processing duration and verification steps, and this causes users' troubles. So for developing reliable and user-friendly biometric system, we fuse soft and primary biometrics to improve the overall performance of the primary biometric system.

Soft biometrics inherit the nonintrusiveness and computational efficiency, which allow for fast, enrolment-free, and pose-invariant biometric analysis. However biometric system based on soft biometric trait only cannot provide accurate recognition because they change over time and lack distinctiveness, so there are still many challenges in this area. Parameter tuning as fusion rules and decision threshold otherwise error rate will increase and this can be improved using fuzzy logic.

Soft biometrics are very sensitive to illumination, expression variations, and pose variation, so we can use deep learning for preprocessing and feature extraction. New soft biometric traits can be also introduced as relative between the size of the head and body and facial distance measurement.

5. Conclusion

In a holistic survey on soft biometrics for user identification, we have seen that there is no one best biometric technology since it depends on the application requirement. A zero false acceptance rate is needed, for example, in security, and the false rejection rate needs to decrease, but in the civilian application, we need the opposite, so for any biometric system, we need to find a good balance between authentication reliability and complexity. As a result, traditional biometrics suffer from low recognition rate because they need cooperation with the user, operate in the controlled environment, and introduce privacy concern. So using multi-biometrics is the solution, but still, the system suffers from computation cost and long processing steps. However, another possible solution is to use soft biometrics to increase the population coverage and decrease the system cost and complexity.

http://dx.doi.org/10.5772/intechopen.76021

Author details

Abdelgader Abdelwhab[1] and Serestina Viriri[2]*

*Address all correspondence to: viriris@ukzn.ac.za

1 College of Computer Science and Information Technology, Sudan University of Science and Technology, Khartoum, Sudan

2 School of Maths, Statistics and Computer Science, University of KwaZulu-Natal, Durban, South Africa

References

[1] Zhang DD. Automated Biometrics: Technologies and Systems. Vol. 7. Berlin: Springer Science & Business Media; 2013

[2] Shoniregun CA. The future of internet security. Ubiquity. 2002;**2002**:8

[3] Clarke R. Human identification in information systems: Management challenges and public policy issues. Information Technology & People. 1994;**7**(4):6-37

[4] Srinivasa K, Gosukonda S. Continuous multimodal user authentication: Coupling hard and soft biometrics with support vector machines to attenuate noise. CSI transactions on ICT. 2014;**2**(2):129-140

[5] Franke K, Ruiz-del-Solar J, Koppen M. Soft-biometrics: Soft-computing for biometric-applications. International Journal of Fuzzy Systems. 2002;**4**(2):665

[6] Lu X, Jain AK. Ethnicity identification from face images. In: Defense and Security. International Society for Optics and Photonics; 2004. pp. 114-123

[7] Jain AK, Ross A, Prabhakar S. An introduction to biometric recognition. IEEE Transactions on Circuits and Systems for Video Technology. 2004;**14**(1):4-20

[8] Jain A, Verma CK. A framework based on hybrid biometrics for personal verification systems. International Journal of Applied. 2012;**1**(1):55-58

[9] Kim M-G, Moon H-M, Chung Y, Pan SB. A survey and proposed framework on the soft biometrics technique for human identification in intelligent video surveillance system. BioMed Research International. 2012;**2012**

[10] Jain AK, Dass SC, Nandakumar K. Can soft biometric traits assist user recognition? In: Defense and Security. International Society for Optics and Photonics; 2004. pp. 561-572

[11] Jain AK, Park U. Facial marks: Soft biometric for face recognition. In: 2009 16th IEEE International Conference on Image Processing (ICIP). IEEE; 2009. pp. 37-40

[12] Dantcheva A, Elia P, Ross A. What else does your biometric data reveal? A survey on soft biometrics. IEEE Transactions on Information Forensics and Security. 2016;**11**(3):441-467

[13] Jain AK, Dass SC, Nandakumar K. Soft biometric traits for personal recognition systems. In: Zhang D, Jain AK, editors. Biometric Authentication. Berlin/Heidelberg: Springer; 2004. pp. 731-738

[14] Zewail R, Elsafi A, Saeb M, Hamdy N. Soft and hard biometrics fusion for improved identity verification. In: The 2004 47th Midwest Symposium on Circuits and Systems, 2004. MWSCAS'04. Vol. 1. IEEE; 2004. pp. I-225

[15] Khalifa AB, BenAmara NE. Contribution to the fusion of biometric modalities by the choquet integral. International Journal of Image, Graphics and Signal Processing. 2012;**4**(10):1

[16] Frischholz RW, Dieckmann U. Biold: A multimodal biometric identification system. Computer. 2000;**33**(2):64-68

[17] Sree SRS, Radha N. A survey on fusion techniques for multimodal biometric identification. International Journal of Innovative Research in Computer. 2014:7493-7497

[18] Sanderson C, Paliwal KK. Information fusion and person verification using speech and face information. Research Paper IDIAP-RR; 2002. pp. 02-33

[19] Ross A, Poh N. Multibiometric systems: Overview, case studies, and open issues. In: Tistarelli M, Li SZ, Chellappa R, editors. Handbook of Remote Biometrics. Berlin: Springer; 2009. pp. 273-292

[20] Jain A, Nandakumar K, Ross A. Score normalization in multimodal biometric systems. Pattern Recognition. 2005;**38**(12):2270-2285

[21] Hicklin A, Ulery B, Watson C. A Brief Introduction to Biometric Fusion. National Institute of Standards and Technology; 2006

[22] Ho TK, Hull J, Srihari SN, Senior Member. Decision combination in multiple classifier systems. Analysis. 1994;**16**(I):66-75

[23] Lam L, Suen SY. Application of majority voting to pattern recognition: An analysis of its behavior and performance. IEEE Transactions on Systems, Man, and Cybernetics Part A: Systems and Humans. 1997;**27**(5):553-568

[24] Achermann B, Bunke H. Combination of Classifiers on the Decision Level for Face Recognition Combination of Classifiers on the Decision Level for Face Recognition, January; 1996

[25] Zadeh LA. I. Introduction, and U. S. Navy, Fuzzy Sets * -, vol. 353; 1965. pp. 338-353

[26] Cavadini D, Fasel AMD, Cimasoni L. Introducing the biometrical electronic passport (epass); 2006

[27] Shen W, Tan T. Automated biometrics-based personal identification. Proceedings of the National Academy of Sciences. 1999;**96**(20):11065-11066

[28] Tome P, Fierrez J, Vera-Rodriguez R, Nixon MS. Soft biometrics and their application in person recognition at a distance. IEEE Transactions on Information Forensics and Security. 2014;**9**(3):464-475

[29] Lee J-E, Jain AK, Jin R. Scars, marks, and tattoos (smt): Soft biometric for the suspect and victim identification. In: Biometrics Symposium, 2008. BSYM'08. IEEE; 2008. pp. 1-8

[30] Ran Y, Rosenbush G, Zheng Q. Computational approaches for real-time extraction of soft biometrics. In: 19th International Conference on Pattern Recognition, ICPR 2008. IEEE; 2008. pp. 1-4 December

[31] Denman S, Fookes C, Bialkowski A, Sridharan S. Soft biometrics: Unconstrained authentication in a surveillance environment. In: Digital Image Computing: Techniques and Applications, 2009. DICTA'09. IEEE; 2009. pp. 196-203

[32] Denman S, Fookes C, Bialkowski A, Sridharan S. Soft-biometrics: Unconstrained authentication in a surveillance environment. In: Digital Image Computing: Techniques and Applications, IEEE 2009. DICTA'09. 2009. pp. 196-203

[33] Niinuma K, Park U, Jain AK. Soft biometric traits for continuous user authentication. IEEE Transactions on Information Forensics and Security. 2010;**5**(4):771-780

[34] Park U, Jain AK. Face matching and retrieval using soft biometrics. IEEE Transactions on Information Forensics and Security. 2010;**5**(3):406-415

[35] Dantcheva A, Dugelay J-L, Elia P. Person recognition using a bag of facial soft biometrics (bofsb). In: 2010 IEEE International Workshop on Multimedia Signal Processing (MMSP). IEEE; 2010. pp. 511-516

[36] Saini N, Sinha A. Soft biometrics in conjunction with optics based biohashing. Optics Communications. 2011;**284**(3):756-763

[37] Min R, Hadid A, Dugelay J-L. Improving the recognition of faces occluded by facial accessories. In: 2011 IEEE International Conference on Automatic Face & Gesture Recognition and Workshops (FG 2011). IEEE; 2011. pp. 442-447

[38] Velardo C, Dugelay J-L. Improving identification by pruning: A case study on face recognition and body soft biometric. In: 2012 13th International Workshop on Image Analysis for Multimedia Interactive Services (WIAMIS). IEEE; 2012. pp. 1-4

[39] Tiwari S, Singh A, Singh SK. Integrating faces and soft-biometrics for newborn recognition. International Journal of Advanced Computer Engineering and Architecture. 2012;**2**(2):201-209

[40] Ghalleb AEK, Sghaier S, Amara NEB. Face recognition improvement using soft biometrics. In: 2013 10th International Multi-Conference on Systems, Signals & Devices (SSD). IEEE; 2013. pp. 1-6

[41] Nazre B, Taheri S, Chellappa R. Assessment of facial wrinkles as a soft biometrics. In: 2013 10th IEEE International Conference and Workshops on Automatic Face and Gesture Recognition (FG). 2013. pp. 1-7

[42] Almudhahka N, Nixon M, Hare J. Human face identification via comparative soft biometrics. In: 2016 IEEE International Conference on Identity, Security and Behavior Analysis (ISBA). IEEE; 2016. pp. 1-6

[43] Jaha ES, Nixon MS. Soft biometrics for subject identification using clothing attributes. In: 2014 IEEE International Joint Conference on Biometrics (IJCB). 2014. pp. 1-6

[44] Chen Q, Huang J, Feris R, Brown LM, Dong J, Yan S. Deep Domain Adaptation for Describing People Based on Fine-Grained Clothing Attributes; 2015. pp. 5315-5324

[45] Zhu J, Liao S, Yi D, Lei Z, Li SZ. Multi-label CNN based pedestrian attribute learning for soft biometrics. In: Proceedings of 2015 International Conference on Biometrics, ICB 2015;**2015**. pp. 535-540

[46] Almudhahka NY, Nixon MS, Hare JS. Automatic semantic face recognition. In: 2017 12th IEEE International Conference on Automatic Face and Gesture Recognition (FG 2017); 2017. pp. 180-185

[47] Lin D, Tang X. Recognize high resolution faces: From macrocosm to microcosm. In: 2006 IEEE Computer Society Conference on Computer Vision and Pattern Recognition. Vol. 2. IEEE; 2006. pp. 1355-1362

[48] Dantcheva A, Velardo C, Dangelo A, Dugelay J-L. Bag of soft biometrics for person identification. Multimedia Tools and Applications. 2011;**51**(2):739-777

[49] An L, Chen X, Kafai M, Yang S, Bhanu B. Improving person re-identification by soft biometrics based reranking. In: 2013 7th International Conference on Distributed Smart Cameras, ICDSC 2013;**2013**. pp. 4-9

Face Recognition with Facial Occlusion Based on Local Cycle Graph Structure Operator

Jucheng Yang, Lingchao Zhang, Meng Li,
Tingting Zhao, Yarui Chen, Jianzheng Liu and Na Liu

Additional information is available at the end of the chapter

http://dx.doi.org/10.5772/intechopen.78597

Abstract

Facial occlusion is a difficulty in the field of face recognition. The lack of features caused by occlusion may reduce the face recognition rate greatly. How to extract the identified features from the occluded faces has a profound effect on face recognition. This chapter presents a Local Cycle Graph Structure (LCGS) operator, which makes full use of the information of the pixels around the target pixel with its neighborhood of 3 × 3. Thus, the recognition with the extracted features is more efficient. We apply the extreme learning machine (ELM) classifier to train and test the features extracted by LCGS algorithm. In the experiment, we use the olivetti research laboratory (ORL) database to simulate occlusion randomly and use the AR database for physical occlusion. Physical coverings include scarves and sunglasses. Experimental results demonstrate that our algorithm yields a state-of-the-art performance.

Keywords: face recognition, facial occlusion, local cycle graph structure

1. Introduction

With the development of science and technology, face recognition technology gradually appeared in our daily life. As the unique biometric key [1], people can use it as a password to protect personal property and information security; the police can arrest criminals through scanning faces based on the photos obtained from cameras [2]. All these applications require face recognition technology. However, most of the faces collected in those practical applications are occluded in some dynamic environments, such as scarves, sunglasses, and so on.

Thus, extracting the effective facial feature information from the occluded faces is the key issue for face recognition.

Many feature extraction algorithms have been proposed to extract facial features; the extracted features can be divided into global features [3] and local features [4–6]. It has been shown that the extracted global facial features cannot effectively solve the recognition problems with occluded faces [7]. On the other hand, local features could deal with face recognition with occluded faces fairly well.

Abusham et al. [8] proposed the Local Graph Structure (LGS) operator, which combines 5 pixels around the center pixel into a graph structure in the neighborhood of 3 × 4. The LGS algorithm improves the recognition rate through the efficient use of pixel information in the neighborhood. However, the graph structure constructed by the LGS algorithm is unbalanced. Abdullah et al. [9] proposed a Symmetric Local Graph Structure (SLGS) algorithm to solve the unbalanced problem. However, SLGS only considers the pixel information on the left and right sides of the target pixel without analyzing the information in other directions. Thus, the information in the extracted features is still insufficient to achieve a good recognition rate. For this issue, Dong et al. [10] proposed MOW-SLGS algorithm, which calculates the characteristic value of pixels around the target pixel in the 5 × 5 neighborhood in the direction of 0, 45, 90, and 135°, respectively, and gives the optimal weight. Finally, the maximum value of the four directions is set as the eigenvalue. MOW-SLGS was shown to provide a reasonable recognition rate.

However, LGS and MOW-SLGS only choose several pixels in the neighborhood of 3 × 4 and 5 × 5. When computing the feature values, they do not consider all the pixels. This will lead to some information loss. To solve this problem, this chapter proposes a Local Cycle Graph Structure (LCGS) operator, which constructs the graph structure in the neighborhood of 3 × 3. The feature values of the target pixel are obtained by using all the pixels in its selected neighborhood. Due to the dimension of the matrix of the characteristic values is too large, the training for classification is not easy. Therefore, we employ the principal component analysis (PCA) [11, 12] method for dimensionality reduction through the experiments. We use the extreme learning machine (ELM) [13, 14] to classify and match the features after dimensionality reduction. Experimental results show that the LCGS algorithm performs better for face recognition with occlusion.

The rest of this article is organized as follows. Section 2 introduces the technical details of LGS and MOW-SLGS; Section 3 gives the detailed algorithm of LCGS; Section 4 shows the experimental results on the ORL and AR database; Section 5 concludes this manuscript.

2. Related theory

2.1. Local graph structure (LGS)

LGS algorithm [8] applied the graph structure in the calculation of the feature values, the main idea is as follows: take the center pixel as the target pixel, and take the two pixels of the left side and three pixels of the right side in the neighborhood of 3 × 4 to constitute the graph structure. Then compare the pixel value of the target pixel and its two pixels on the left by the counterclockwise. Set to 1 when the pixel value becomes larger, to 0 when it becomes smaller. Three pixels on the right side of the target pixel are compared in the clockwise direction. The same as above, set to 1 when the pixel value becomes larger, to 0 when it becomes smaller. Finally, the target pixel value is compared with the adjacent pixel value on the right. The whole procedure is shown in **Figure 1**, where X_0 is the target pixel. The comparison order is conducted as $X_0 \to X_1 \to X_2 \to X_0 \to X_3 \to X_4 \to X_5 \to X_3 \to X_0$. The final result is composed by these eight binary numbers. Finally, we convert the 8-bit binary numbers to its decimal format.

A specific example of LGS operator is shown in **Figure 1**. By comparing the value of the pixel with its adjacent pixel along the direction of arrows, the binary value of X_0 is 10,001,011. As a result, the decimal value of the target pixel is obtained as 139.

2.2. Multi-orientation weighted symmetric local graph structure (MOW-SLGS)

MOW-SLGS algorithm [10] is improved based on the LGS algorithm, which mitigates the problems of the LGS algorithm by constructing the graph structure in the horizontal direction. The extracted feature for the target pixel is not sufficient, and the weight ratio is not balanced. The algorithm is implemented as follows: in the 5 × 5 neighborhood, we take the center pixel as the target pixel, and then the graph structure is constructed by the target pixel in 0, 45, 90, and 135° direction. Finally, we calculate the feature values of each direction. For the directions of 0, 45, and 135°, the left side of the target pixel is used to compare the value of the pixel in the counterclockwise direction, the right side of the target pixel to compare the value of the pixel in the clockwise direction. If the pixel value is larger, we set it to 1; otherwise set 0. For the direction of 90°, the comparison of the upper side of the target pixel with counter-clockwise order, the lower side of the target pixel with the counter-clockwise order. The binary value is read from the central pixel along each direction. Each direction is firstly in the counter-clockwise order, and then in the clockwise order. The weight of the 8-bit binary number obtained by the algorithm of MOW-SLGS in each direction is shown in **Figure 2**, where X_0 is the target pixel. Finally, the maximum value is obtained as the characteristic value.

We take the direction of 45° as the example as shown in **Figure 3**. It can be seen that the characteristic value of the target pixel in the direction of 45° is 01101101. Thus, the final value is 122 after calculating its corresponding decimal value.

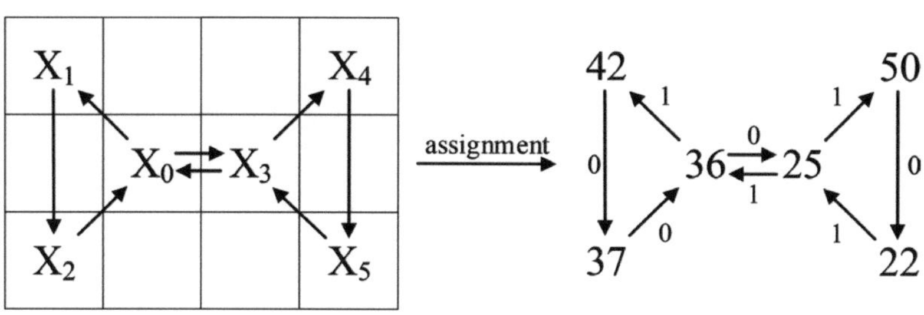

Figure 1. Template of LGS operator and its example.

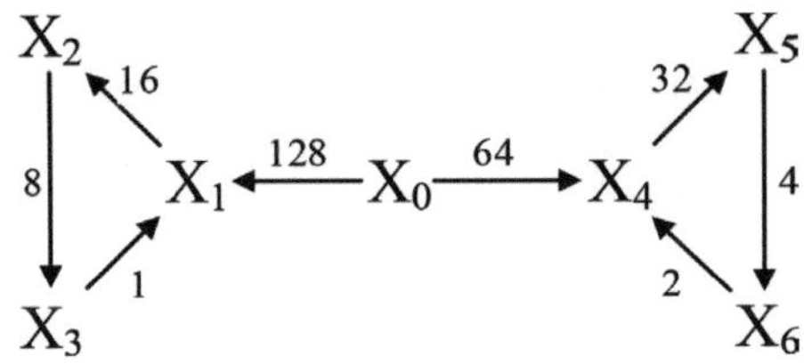

Figure 2. The design of weights for MOW-SLGS.

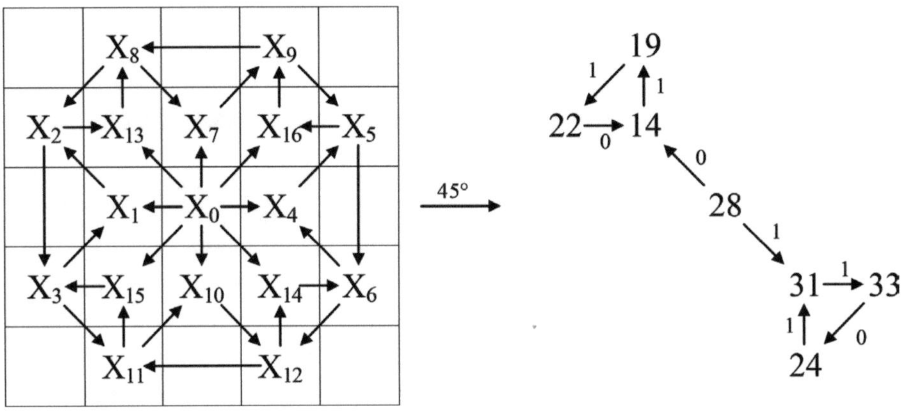

Figure 3. Graph structure of MOW-SLGS in the direction of 45°.

3. Proposed method

The characteristic value of the target pixel extracted by LGS and MOW-SLGS algorithm are in the neighborhood of 3 × 4 and 5 × 5. It can be seen that these two algorithms do not consider all the surrounding pixels in the neighborhood. This leads to the lack of information about the surrounding pixels, which will have an impact on the recognition rate.

In order to solve this problem, we propose a LCGS algorithm by using the full information of the surrounding pixels. In such way, LCGS can get more representative features for the target pixels, thus, improve the recognition rate.

The way to extract the characteristics of the face image with LCGS algorithm is illustrated in **Figure 4**.

In **Figure 4**, the center pixel X_0 is taken as the target pixel in the neighborhood of 3 × 3. The remaining pixels are represented by X_1 to X_8, respectively. We put all the pixels in accordance with $X_0 \rightarrow X_8 \rightarrow X_1 \rightarrow X_0$, $X_0 \rightarrow X_2 \rightarrow X_3 \rightarrow X_0$, $X_0 \rightarrow X_4 \rightarrow X_5 \rightarrow X_0$, $X_0 \rightarrow X_6 \rightarrow X_7 \rightarrow X_0$ to compare the value of the pixel. If the value of the pixel is larger in the direction of the arrow, we set it to 1; otherwise, we set it to 0. Finally, we obtain 12 binary numbers in sequence from $X_0 \rightarrow X_8$ to $X_7 \rightarrow X_0$. The decimal format of these 12 binary values is the characteristic value. A specific example is shown in **Figure 5**.

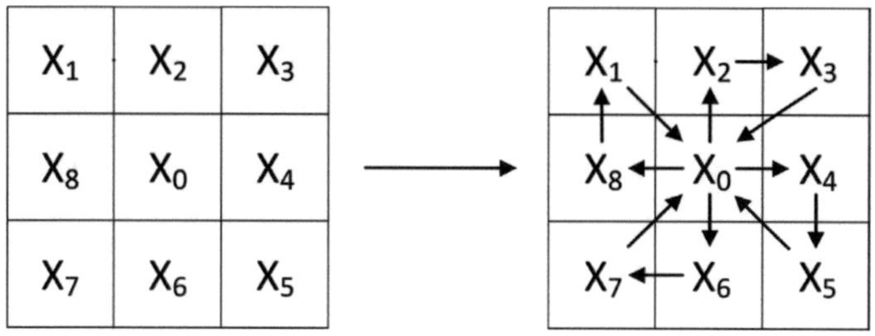

Figure 4. LCGS operator.

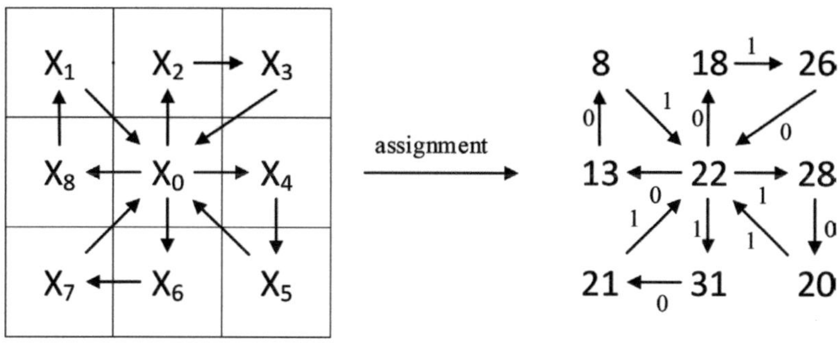

Figure 5. Template of LCGS operator.

In **Figure 5**, we calculate the characteristic value according to our proposed LCGS algorithm. The target pixel value is 22. The value of target pixel is 22. We compare the value of pixels in according to the order of $X_0 \rightarrow X_8 \rightarrow X_1 \rightarrow X_0 \rightarrow X_2 \rightarrow X_3 \rightarrow X_0 \rightarrow X_4 \rightarrow X_5 \rightarrow X_0 \rightarrow X_6 \rightarrow X_7 \rightarrow X_0$, and get the binary values as 001010101101. It is converted to the decimal number, that is, F (X_0) $=0 \times 2048 + 0 \times 1024 + 1 \times 512 + 0 \times 256 + 1 \times 128 + 0 \times 64 + 1 \times 32 + 0 \times 16 + 1 \times 8 + 1 \times 4 + 0 \times 2 + 1 \times 1 = 685$, which gives the final feature values for the target pixel.

In the LCGS algorithm, we define the neighborhood of 3×3 along the traditional way. It is effective to calculate the characteristic values of the target pixel by considering all the surrounding pixels in the neighborhood. Thus, it makes the final recognition rate improved.

4. Experiments and analysis

In order to investigate the reliability of LCGS algorithm, we use the AR physical occlusion database and the ORL simulation occlusion database to conduct the experiments. The AR face database consists of 126 people, a total of 3276 images, 26 pictures per person. The 26 pictures are collected in two different time periods, including changes in light, occlusion, and so on. The shelter is divided into scarves and sunglasses. The ORL Face Database was created by the University of Cambridge AT &T Lab, which contains 40 people, 10 images per person, and a total of 400 face images. We use a baboon image to randomly block the original image for the occlusion simulation. Some examples of AR database and ORL database are shown in **Figures 6** and **7**.

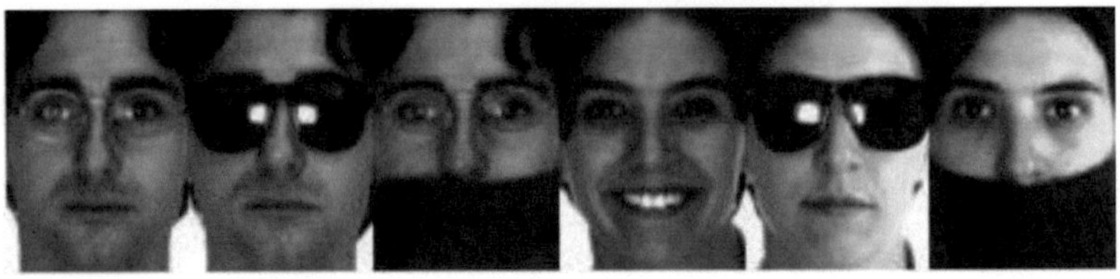

Figure 6. Examples of AR face database.

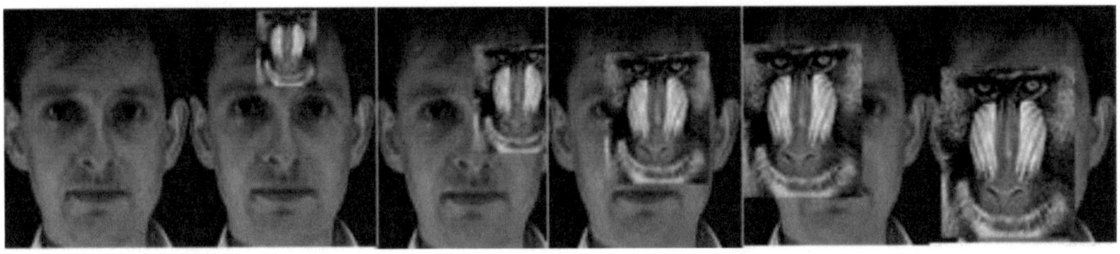

Figure 7. Examples of ORL face database.

4.1. Dimensionality reduction using principal component analysis (PCA)

The LCGS algorithm is used to extract the features of a face image, and the dimension of the feature matrix is usually very large, which makes it difficult to use the classifier to train and test. Therefore, we adopt a state-of-the-art method Principal Component Analysis (PCA) [11, 12] to reduce the dimension after feature extraction. For the implementation of PCA, we set the principal component contribution rate as 0.95.

4.2. Training and classification using extreme learning machine (ELM)

In the stage of image classification, we employ the Extreme Learning Machine (ELM) [13, 14] to train and classify the data. This algorithm is a supervised learning algorithm for single-hidden layer feed-forward network (SLFN). The main idea of ELM is to determine the number of hidden layer neurons, then perform random assignment on the input weights and hidden layer bias, and finally the output layer weights can be directly calculated by the least squares method. The entire learning process is completed at once, without iteration, so its learning speed is very fast. Based on the extensive experimental experience, we set the number of hidden layer nodes to 2000.

4.3. The experimental results

4.3.1. Experimental results on AR face database

In this section, we compared the LCGS algorithm with the traditional LGS, SLGS and MOW-SLGS algorithms in terms of recognition rate on AR face database. Hundred people in the database are selected as our experimental data, where half of men and women. The training set selects unobstructed face images, seven images per person, and a total of 700 images. The test set is divided into three parts. The shelter in test data set 1 is a scarf, three images per

Test set	LGS	SLGS	MOW-SLGS	LCGS
Test set 1 (scarf)	0.8367	0.8847	0.8967	0.9127
Test set 2 (sunglasses)	0.8970	0.9413	0.9380	0.9533
Test set 3 (scarf + sunglasses)	0.8620	0.9147	0.9203	0.9295

Table 1. Recognition rates of different algorithms on the AR database.

person, a total of 300 images. The shelter in test data set 2 is sunglasses, three images per person, a total of 300 images. The shelter in test set 3 is a mixture of scarves and sunglasses, each with six images, a total of 300 images. The results of the recognition rates are shown in **Table 1**.

Through **Table 1**, we can see that recognition rate achieved by LCGS algorithm is higher than other algorithms for all these three test data set. In particular, when the shelter of the test set is a scarf, the recognition rates of the LGS, SLGS, and MOW-SLGS algorithms are 83.67, 88.47, and 89.67%. Moreover, the recognition rate of the LCGS algorithm is 91.27%, which well demonstrates the advantages of our proposed method in the occluded images with a scarf. We also find that the recognition rate for test set 1 is the lowest among the three test data sets. This is due to the occlusion caused by the scarf almost accounted for 20% of the image. It has a great effect on the feature extraction of the whole image.

4.3.2. Experimental results on ORL face database

We performed an analog occlusion experiment on the ORL face database, and we chose LGS, SLGS, and MOW-SLGS to compare our proposed algorithm, LCGS. We used a baboon picture to block the original face picture randomly. We set the occlusion area as 10%, 20%, 30%, 40%, and 50% of the original image. We set up three training sets. The first group selected six images per person, a total of 240 images. The second group selects seven images per person, a total of 280 images. The third group selects eight images per person, a total of 320 images. Corresponding, the test set is also divided into three groups. The test set 1 is four images per person, a total of 160 images. The test set 2 is three images per person, a total of 120 images. The test set 3 is two images per person, a total of 80 images. The results are shown in **Table 2**, **Figure 8**, and **Table 3**.

Occlusion area (%)	LGS	SLGS	MOW-SLGS	LCGS
10	0.5425	0.5731	0.6375	0.6713
20	0.5156	0.5531	0.6188	0.6275
30	0.4587	0.5300	0.5587	0.6019
40	0.3625	0.4450	0.4731	0.5063
50	0.2863	0.3606	0.3775	0.4044

Table 2. Recognition rates of different algorithms on test set 1 of the ORL database.

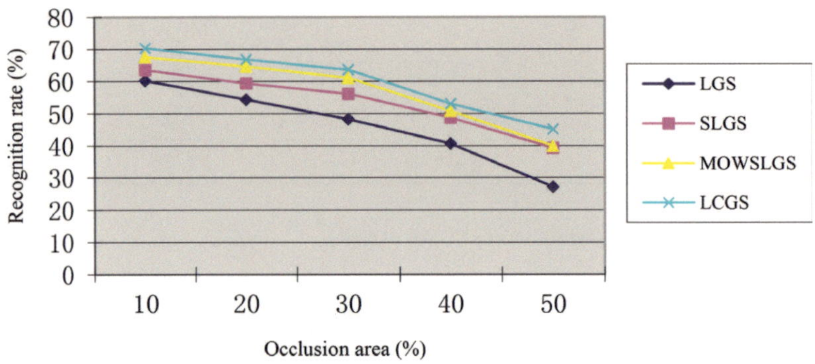

Figure 8. Recognition rates of different algorithms on test set 2 of the ORL database.

Occlusion area (%)	LGS	SLGS	MOW-SLGS	LCGS
10	0.5700	0.5988	0.6975	0.7013
20	0.5362	0.5838	0.6663	0.6738
30	0.4900	0.5688	0.5925	0.6200
40	0.4025	0.4763	0.5275	0.5463
50	0.2888	0.4113	0.3825	0.4188

Table 3. Recognition rates of different algorithms on test set 3 of the ORL database.

From **Table 2**, **Figure 8**, and **Table 3**, we can clearly see that the recognition rate of the LCGS algorithm is higher than that of the conventional algorithms. In the test set 1, the recognition rates of the LGS, SLGS, and MOW-SLGS algorithms are 45.87%, 53.00% and 55.87%, respectively, when the occlusion area is 30%, and the recognition rate of the LCGS algorithm is 60.19%.

4.3.3. *10-fold cross-validation*

In order to further verify the accuracy of the algorithm, we also conducted 10-fold cross-validation. We chose the ORL database and randomly masked only one piece of data for testing. The comparison algorithms are LGS, SLGS, and MOW-SLGS. The result is shown in **Table 4**.

Through the experimental results, as shown in **Table 4**, we can see that LCGS algorithm performs better than other algorithms. The recognition rates of the LGS, SLGS, and MOW-SLGS algorithms are 49.00%, 53.00%, and 55.25%, respectively, when the occlusion area is 40% while the recognition rate of the LCGS algorithm is 61.75%.

4.3.4. *Comparison of the processing time*

During the experiments, we compared the processing time for the same image required by the LGS, SLGS, MOW-SLGS, and our proposed LCGS algorithm. The result is shown in **Table 5**.

Occlusion area (%)	LGS	SLGS	MOW-SLGS	LCGS
10	0.6900	0.7150	0.7875	0.7825
20	0.6850	0.6900	0.7475	0.7575
30	0.5650	0.6400	0.6875	0.6925
40	0.4900	0.5300	0.5525	0.6175
50	0.3625	0.4675	0.4275	0.5200

Table 4. 10-fold cross-validation experiment results for different algorithms.

Algorithms	LGS	SLGS	MOW-SLGS	LCGS
Processing time (second)	0.2886	0.2895	1.0093	0.4493

Table 5. The processing time of different algorithms.

Through **Table 5**, we can see that the processing time required for one image by the LCGS algorithm is 0.4493 seconds. Although the required time is higher than that of LGS and SLGS, it is significantly less than the time required by the MOW-SLGS. The reason is that the MOW-SLGS algorithm calculates the feature values of the four directions around the target pixel. Each direction is located on both sides of the target pixel, that is, a total of eight sets of feature values are calculated. The proposed LCGS algorithm only calculates the four sets of feature values based on the full usage of the surrounding pixels. Therefore, MOW-SLGS's processing time is about twice as high as LCGS.

5. Conclusion

In this chapter, we proposed a LCGS algorithm and applied it to face recognition with occlusion. LCGS makes full use of the texture features of the surrounding pixels in the 3 × 3 neighborhood. It makes up for the shortcomings of LGS and MOW-SLGS algorithm where the information around the target pixel is not sufficient. The characteristics of the target pixel value using LCGS algorithm is easier to recognize. Therefore, it improves the recognition rates with occlusion. Through the experiments on the AR and ORL database, we demonstrated that the LCGS algorithm is superior to the traditional algorithm in the recognition rate of face images with occlusion, and the time consumption is lower than the MOW-SLGS algorithm.

Acknowledgements

This work was supported by the National Natural Science Foundation of China under Grant No.61502338 and No. 61502339, the 2015 key projects of Tianjin science and technology support program No. 15ZCZDGX00200, the Project of Scientific Research Plan of Tianjin Education Committee NO.2017KJ034, and Tianjin Food Safety & Low Carbon Manufacturing Collaborative Innovation Center.

Author details

Jucheng Yang, Lingchao Zhang, Meng Li, Tingting Zhao*, Yarui Chen, Jianzheng Liu and Na Liu

*Address all correspondence to: tingting@tust.edu.cn

College of Computer Science and Information Engineering, Tianjin University of Science and Technology, Tianjin, China

References

[1] Kumar A, Zhou Y. Human identification using finger images. IEEE Transactions on Image Processing. 2012;**21**(4):2228-2244

[2] Ahonen T, Hadid A, Pietikainen M. Face description with local binary patterns: Application to face recognition. IEEE Transactions on Pattern Analysis and Machine Intelligence. 2006;**28**(12):2037-2041

[3] Yu H, Yang J. A direct LDA algorithm for high-dimensional data—With application to face recognition. Pattern Recognition. 2001;**34**(10):2067-2070

[4] Ojala T, Pietikainen M, Harwood D. Performance evaluation of texture measures with classification based on Kullback discrimination of distributions. In: Pattern Recognition, 1994. Proceedings of the 12th IAPR International Conference on Conference A: Computer Vision & Image Processing. Vol. 1. Jerusalem, Israel: IEEE; 1994. pp. 582-585

[5] Ojala T, Pietikainen M, Maenpaa T. Multiresolution gray-scale and rotation invariant texture classification with local binary patterns. IEEE Transactions on Pattern Analysis and Machine Intelligence. 2002;**24**(7):971-987

[6] Tan X, Triggs B. Enhanced local texture feature sets for face recognition under difficult lighting conditions. IEEE Transactions on Image Processing. 2010;**19**(6):1635-1650

[7] Li X-X, Liang R. A review for face recognition with occlusion: From subspace regression to deep learning. Chinese Journal of Computers. 2017;**40**:82

[8] Abusham EE, Bashir HK. Face recognition using local graph structure (LGS). In: International Conference on Human-Computer Interaction. Berlin, Heidelberg: Springer; 2011. pp. 169-175

[9] Abdullah MFA, Sayeed MS, Muthu KS, Bashier HK, Azman A, Ibrahim SZ. Face recognition with symmetric local graph structure (slgs). Expert Systems with Applications. 2014;**41**(14):6131-6137

[10] Dong S, Yang J, Chen Y, Wang C, Zhang X, Park DS. Finger vein recognition based on multi-orientation weighted symmetric local graph structure. KSII Transactions on Internet and Information Systems. 2015;**9**(10):4126-4142

[11] Luo Y, Zhang T, Zhang Y. A novel fusion method of PCA and LDP for facial expression feature extraction. Optik-International Journal for Light and Electron Optics. 2016;**127**(2):718-721

[12] Turk M, Pentland A. Eigenfaces for recognition. Journal of Cognitive Neuroscience. 1991;**3**(1):71-86

[13] Huang G-B, Zhu Q-Y, Siew C-K. Extreme learning machine: Theory and applications. Neurocomputing. 2006;**70**(1):489-501

[14] Zong W, Huang G-B. Face recognition based on extreme learning machine. Neurocomputing. 2011;**74**(16):2541-2551

Section 2

Machine Learning for Biometrics

Chapter 5

Electrocardiogram Recognization Based on Variational AutoEncoder

Shaojie Chen, Zhaopeng Meng and Qing Zhao

Additional information is available at the end of the chapter

http://dx.doi.org/10.5772/intechopen.76434

Abstract

Subtle distortions on electrocardiogram (ECG) can help doctors to diagnose some serious larvaceous heart sickness on their patients. However, it is difficult to find them manually because of disturbing factors such as baseline wander and high-frequency noise. In this chapter, we propose a method based on variational autoencoder to distinguish these distortions automatically and efficiently. We test our method on three ECG datasets from Physionet by adding some tiny artificial distortions. Comparing with other approaches adopting autoencoders [e.g., contractive autoencoder, denoising autoencoder (DAE)], the results of our experiment show that our method improves the performance of publically available on ECG analysis on the distortions.

Keywords: electrocardiogram, variational autoencoder, variational inference, ECG enhancement, deep learning

1. Introduction

Automatic electrocardiogram (ECG) recognition [29] is greatly helpful to doctors in their diagnosis and treatment of heart disease. As the number of portable ECG devices is increasing, more and more ECG records are available. However, it is inevitable that these ECG data are contaminated by different kinds of noise caused by such interference as baseline wandering, muscle shaking, and electrode movement [13, 14]. Considering the level and complexity of these noises, especially those components that may cause subtle deformations on ECG waveforms, these factors may decrease the accuracy of the ECG recognition. Additionally, there are much more unlabeled ECG data (i.e., there are not any type information about the data) that are stored in a lot of databases. Therefore, it is necessary to improve the performance of automatic ECG classification in unsupervised context by choosing proper models and algorithms.

In order to prevent noisy inference, many approaches of preprocessing or enhancement of ECG were successfully employed to remove the contaminations. Traditionally, most of these approaches are based on the filtering technology on frequency domain. Ziarani et al. and Konrad [15] eliminated the power line noise by extracting a specified component of a signal and tracking its variations over time. Alfaouri et.al. [16] and Dewangan et al. [17] employed wavelet transform method to isolate baseline wander and effectively detect and suppress the presence of power line interference in ECG. Although these filters can help suppress the high-frequency interference, they may drop out some useful information on the heart illness simultaneously. Because the frequency spectrum spreads not only low band but also high band. To overcome these drawbacks of filtering-based methods, some adaptive methods have been proposed. Abdelmounim et al. [18] applied adaptive algorithm to remove those noise that subsequently adapt to the wavelets selected by proper thresholding. However, the author also reported that this method had its own relative disadvantage that it had incapability of removing baseline wandering smoothly and effectively. Additionally, other technologies such as Fourier transform (FT) and empirical mode decomposition (EMD) were also employed for ECG preprocessing [19, 20]. FT maps the higher frequency components into the low area. Similarly, EMD separates different ECG components by proper intrinsic mode functions.

Feature extraction is another important procedure of ECG recognition. ECG features consists of amplitudes, intervals, and segments, which are shown in **Figure 1**. Each feature indicates certain activities of heart. For example, P wave represents atrial depolarization, it causes both atria to contract and pump blood to ventricles. Any distortion of P wave indicates malfunction of atrial appears.

Traditionally, the goal of ECG feature extraction is to extract all abovementioned features. As the amplitude of R wave is much larger than any others, many approaches based on the QRS complex detection have been proposed. Chan et al. [21] used a specific template to match the preferred ECG signals by the computation of the correlation between them. Krasteva and Jekova et al. [22] successfully implemented this method to evaluate the heart

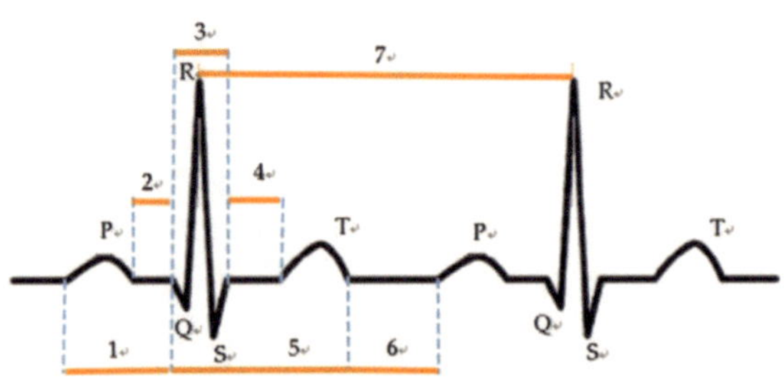

Figure 1. An ECG waveform with two cardiac periods. It consists of P wave, QRS complex, and T wave. Additionally, there are two intervals: PR interval (3) and QT interval (5). Three segments include PR segment (2), ST segment (4), and TP segment (6). RR interval (7) means how long is the duration between two adjacent peaks of R wave.

rhythm. Nevertheless, these approaches are heavily dependent on the prior knowledge about ECG and the relevant areas [23, 25], which cause more difficulties for further applications. Comparatively, some other approaches based on kernel functions are more popular and widely used because of their simplicity and sensitivity. Martis et al. [3] studied several methods [principal component analysis (PCA), linear discriminant analysis (LDA), independent component analysis (ICA), and discrete wavelet transform (DWT)] and compared them in feature extraction for classifying the arrhythmia ECGs. Banerjee et al. [5] focused on two specific regions (QRS complex area and T-wave region) on ECG waveforms to adequately distinguish between normal and abnormal ECG signals by yielding wavelet cross spectrum and wavelet coherence. Kærgaard et al. [6] proposed two hybrid signal processing schemes [ensemble empirical mode decomposition (EEMD) and discrete wavelet transform (DWT)] for ECG features extraction. These schemes were implemented by combining with the neural network and the wavelet transform. Nazarahari et al. [8] chose wavelet functions (WFs) as means of ECG classifying and proposed a wavelet design criterion for wavelet function choosing. Houssein et al. [4] classified the ECG by modified water wave optimization (WWO) algorithms and achieved over 93% average accuracy.

Although many important contributions have been given to ECG feature extraction by conventional methods based on kernel technologies, the accuracy and efficiency of these methods could rarely meet all the requirements of applications especially in the background of noise. Fortunately, different from the kernel methods, neural networks have been used to draw ECG features automatically by the hierarchical structure in the context of deep learning, which could be achieved by a new approach which is known as representation learning. Yan et al. [12] used a restricted Boltzmann machine (RBM) for ECG classification. Xiong et al. [9, 10] employed denoising autoencoder (DAE) and stacked contractive denoising autoencoder for ECG denoising [8], respectively. Zhou et al. [11] chose a stacked sparse autoencoder (SAE) to extract ECG feature for classifying and the level of accuracy achieved by this work shows derivable benefits over the traditional methods that require wavelets transform to perform ECG classification.

In terms of the heart illness automatically diagnosis auxiliary by the ECG recognition, some works mentioned above do not meet the necessary requirements because most studies focused on the arrhythmia distinguishing problems. Nevertheless, many heart diseases have close relationship not only with the rhythms of itself but also with the other features such as the length of the ST segment and the amplitude of P wave on the ECG waveforms. Additionally, there are rarely generative models to be used for ECG recognition. The contributions of this chapter include two aspects: (1) instead of using ECG signals on a cardiac period between two start points at P waves, we propose a new method for intercepting ECG segments between adjacent two R peaks and (2) we use variational autoencoder (VAE) model as an analysis tool to recognize different ECG signals by focusing on the variation of tiny distortion.

This chapter is organized as follows. Section 2 briefly describes autoencoder and its variants. Section 3 introduces the variational inference and variational autoencoder in detail. ECG preprocessing and classifying schema is proposed in Section 4. Our experiment results and discussions are shown in Section 5. Finally, Section 6 concludes.

2. Autoencoders and variants

Variational autoencoder has close relationship with autoencoder. An autoencoder is a neural network that consists of encoder and decoder. Encoder maps its input into representation and decoder reconstructs the representation back into the input, that is, perfect autoencoder can resemble the training data approximately by forcing to prioritize those aspects of the input that are helpful to resembling and discard the others. In this regard, the autoencoder learns the useful properties of training data. Comparatively, VAE shares the same character with AE besides some specialties of its own.

2.1. Autoencoder and regularized variants

Autoencoder can be used to get useful features from the encoder output. Generally, in the view of the feature dimension, autoencoder falls into two categories: undercomplete and overcomplete. Undercomplete means the dimension of feature is less than that of the input and more salient features could be learned well in this scenario. Conversely, in the case of overcomplete, the dimension of feature is greater than that of the input and more sparsity features might be drawn in this setting. Additionally, the objective function is another core topic for an autoencoder. It is designed to make the autoencoder have capabilities such as linear regression or logistic regression, which limit the model to some useful properties of the training data. The general form of the objective function can be depicted as follows:

$$\tilde{J}(X, \theta) = J(X; \theta) + \alpha\Omega(\theta). \tag{1}$$

where X is the training data for a given autoencoder. $\theta = \{W_e, b_e, W_d, b_d\}$ are the parameters of the model and α is a nonnegative hyperparameter that controls how much of the penalty term Ω to the relative to the standard objective function J. Numerically, setting α to 0 means not any regularization and larger values of α result in more regularization. Conceptually, autoencoders with penalty term is usually called regularized autoencoder that is encouraged to have small derivative of the representation, which leads the convergence faster than those that have not any regularization during the training time.

Varied forms of regularizer terms make the autoencoder have different properties and bring us different variants of regularized autoencoder. These variants include primarily sparse autoencoder (SAE), denoising autoencoder (DAE) [3], contractive autoencoder (CAE), and variational autoencoder (VAE). Theoretically, VAE combines variance inference (VI) and neural networks. As a generative model, one of the prominent successes of VAE is that it realizes effective random sampling using back-propagation (BP) technology. This will be described in detail in Section 3.

Different from VAE, SAE makes majority of the neurons in its hidden layers be inactive since the active functions on these neurons are feasibly saturated for most input. This results in the sparsity of features, where many of the elements of the features are zero (or close to zero). In the view of mathematics, the sparsity of SAE is accomplished by the penalty term $KL(\tilde{p}\|p)$, where $\tilde{p}$ is the given sparsity value. Parameter p will be adjusted gradually to $\tilde{p}$ in the training stage and achieve satisfactory sparsity. Analogous to SAE, CAE [4, 26] yields the specialized contractive properties by the penalized term—a Jacobin matrix that is consisted of the partial derivatives of the decoder active functions to input vectors. Then the input perturbations can be resisted during training time. Consequently, neighborhood of points in samples is encouraged to map into a smaller area, which can be thought as the capability of contracting for CAE. The motivation of DAE is to be insensitive to noise. Instead of adding an additional penalty term to the object function, DAE is trained by the noise-corrupted data $\tilde{x}$ ($\tilde{x} = x + \beta\tau$) [27, 30]. DAE yields great success in many cases especially in manifold assumption. As the corrupted data $\tilde{x}$ lie farther away from the manifold than the uncorrupted ones, DAE tends to take those points that are farther from the manifold to near. The larger distance from the manifold, the bigger step DAE takes to the manifold.

Generally, these autoencoders share some properties. DAE and CAE are able to learn the manifold structure of the samples. Simultaneously, SAE and CAE have the similar sparsity character on their representation. Nevertheless, the implementations of these autoencoders are quite different. For example, DAE reaches the goal by using the noise-corrupted data to train the structure to learn the proper parameters that can reconstruct the original samples without any noise. Comparatively, CAE takes Jacobian matrix as part of the loss function and encourages robustness on the representation by contracting the samples during the training process.

3. Variational inference and variational autoencoder

As the central problem in inference analysis, posterior distribution computation is facing two computing challenges: marginal likelihood computation and predictive distribution computation. Both of them are intractable since they often require computing high-dimensional integrals. Therefore, approximate inference approaches such as Gibbs sampling based on Markov chain Monte Carlo (MCMC) principle are appealing. However, Gibbs sampling and its variants are often restricted from some applications for their inefficiencies especially in the high-dimensional scenario. This awkward situation has not been changed until the VAE was proposed theoretically [36]. To get an understanding of a VAE, we will first start from the relevant bases including variational inference (VI), evidence low boundary (ELBO), mean field, and Kullback–Leibler (KL) divergence.

To describe the problem mathematically, let $X = \{x_1, x_2, \ldots, x_N\}$ be a set of N observations and $Z = \{z_1, z_2, \ldots, z_m\}$ be the m latent variables. $P(Z, X; \theta)$ denotes the joint distribution of X and Z given the parameter θ of the model. $P(X \mid Z)$ and $P(Z \mid X)$ are called the likelihood of Z and the posterior distribution of X, respectively.

3.1. Variational inference

Theoretically, the motivation of variational inference [33, 35] is to find a feasible distribution to approximate the desired posterior distribution that is intractable. To measure how closeness of these two distributions are, Kullback–Leibler (KL) divergence [34] is introduced. Let $P(X)$ and $Q(X)$ indicate two different distributions of the continuous random variables X, their KL divergence is defined as:

$$\mathrm{KL}(\mathrm{P}||\mathrm{Q}) = \int Q(X)\, log\frac{Q(X)}{P(X)}\, dX = E_{Q(X)}\left[\log\frac{Q(X)}{P(X)}\right]. \tag{2}$$

Intuitively, KL divergence is nonnegative and monotonically decreasing to the similarity of the distributions, that is, the more similar of the two distributions, the smaller the KL divergence value is. The identity equals zero when $Q(X)$ is the same as $P(X)$. However, the KL divergence is non-symmetrical as $\mathrm{KL}(\mathrm{Q}||\mathrm{P}) \neq \mathrm{KL}(\mathrm{P}||\mathrm{Q})$. The definition indicates implicitly another two properties: the KL divergence equals zero when $Q(X)$ goes infinitively to zero regardless of $P(X)$ and rises asymptotically infinity as $P(X)$ becomes zero. Hence, we can approximate the distribution P(X) for Q(X) by minimizing $\mathrm{KL}(Q(X)\|P(X))$.

3.1.1. *Evidence lower boundary*

In the context of Bayesian statistics, "Evidence" is an alternative term used for the marginal likelihood of the observations. Formula (3) reveals the relationship between KL divergence and the logarithm of the evidence $P(X)$. The difference between them equals the expectation of $\log(p(X, Z)) - \log(q(Z))$, which is called the evidence lower boundary (ELBO). As the KL divergence is nonnegative, then we have the evidence lower boundary as formula (3). Jordan et al. [1] got the same result originally using the Jensen's inequality. Formula (3) shows literally the name of ELBO. We may define the expectation of $\log(p(X, Z)) - \log(q(Z))$ as $L(Q)$, a function of distribution of $Q(Z)$:

$$log(P(X)) - \mathrm{KL}(Q(Z)\|P(Z \mid X)) = E_Q[\log(P(Z, X)) - \log(Q(Z))] \triangleq L(Q). \tag{3}$$

Intuitively, maximizing ELBO is equivalent to minimizing the KL divergence. As the $\mathrm{KL}(Q(Z)\|P(Z \mid X))$ decreases to zero, it is necessary to make the posterior distribution $P(Z \mid X)$ share the same distribution with $Q(Z)$. Hence, we can use $Q(Z)$ to approximate the posterior distribution $P(Z \mid X)$ by maximizing ELBO, which can be realized by optimizing the objective of $L(q)$ as formula (4), finding an optimal distribution $Q^*(Z)$ within a specifying family $\mathcal{Q}$ of densities over the latent variables. Expectation maximization (EM) algorithm [2] is one of the successful approaches that were designed for finding the optimal solution $Q^*(Z)$ within the family $\mathcal{Q}$. It alternates iteratively between expectation step (E-step) where the posterior distribution $P(Z \mid X; \theta)$ is calculated and then, maximization step (M-step) where the expectation of the complete-data likelihood with respect to the posterior distribution $P(Z \mid X; \theta^{old})$ is maximized by optimizing the parameters θ^{new}. Then updates the parameters θ^{old} with θ^{new}:

$$Q^* = \underset{Q \in \mathcal{Q}}{\mathrm{argmax}}\, L(Q). \tag{4}$$

3.1.2. Mean field

To simplify the optimization problem of ELBO, it is necessary to make assumption on the family $\mathcal{Q}$, as the selection of the family affects impressively on complexity of the optimization algorithm for the problem. This assumption focuses on the way that how to factorize $Q(Z)$ as:

$$Q(Z) = \prod_{i=1}^{m} Q_i(Z_i). \tag{5}$$

where $Q_i(Z_i)$ denotes the individual factors that are mutually independent over the latent variables of the model. According to the chain rule of probability, the joint distribution $P(X, Z)$ can be decomposed as:

$$p(Z, X) = p(X) \prod_{i=1}^{m} p(Z_i \mid Z_{1:(i-1)}, X). \tag{6}$$

Then, the ELBO can be written as Eq. (7):

$$L(Q) = \log(P(X)) + \sum_{i=1}^{m} \left(E_Q\left[log\left(P(Z_i \mid Z_{1:(i-1)}, X)\right)\right] - E_{Q_i}\left[\log\left(Q_i(Z_i)\right)\right] \right). \tag{7}$$

where $\log(P(X))$ is constant with respect to $Q(Z)$. Then, maximizing ELBO is equivalently maximizing the last summation term. Furthermore, we can derive out the optimal solution Q^* by Lagrangian multiplier method:

$$Q_i^*(Z_i) \propto \exp\left(E_{-Q_i}\left[log(Z_i, Z_{-i}, X)\right]\right). \tag{8}$$

Formula (8) indicates that the factors are all proportional to the exponentiated log the joint distribution except the ith variational factor. This is the gist of the coordinate ascent variational inference (CAIV) [37] as well. However, as the ELBO is not a necessary convex function, there is no guarantee that the solution Q^* is a global optimum.

3.2. Variational autoencoder

As a deterministic model, general regularized autoencoder does not know anything about how to create a latent vector until a sample is input. Conversely, as a generative model, variational autoencoder (VAE) [36] emerges as a successful example of combination of variance inference and neural network. VAE forces the latent vector following some kind of distribution. These characters not only encourage the properties of the general regularized autoencoders but also expand some additional properties. For example, VAE can generate some data points even without any encoding input. It is the specialty of VAE that differs from the other regularized autoencoders. To explore VAE further, it is necessary to understand those complicated ideas such as the neural network structure, the loss function, and the optimization algorithm.

In the view of the hierarchy, the neural network structure of the VAE is mainly composed of three parts. The first part is the encoder, which is used to encode the signals from the input layer. The second part is the decoder, which is located in the right side as shown in **Figure 2**. The third part is the sampling unit located in the middle of the other two parts. Except for the encoder and the decoder which are similar to that of the traditional autoencoder, the additional sampling unit is responsible for sampling from the latent variables spaces.

Another issue about how to train the structure is the loss function as shown in formula (9), which is essentially the same as the negative $L(Q)$ in formula (7). In the view of training, the losses of a VAE come from two aspects: the first part is from the neural network that measures how much the difference between the reconstructed data and the original input. This part encourages the decoder to learn to reconstruct the input. Otherwise, the value of this part will become even larger that will increase the total loss value finally. The second part comes from the KL divergence that indicates how much close of the encoder's distribution $Q(Z \mid X)$ and the latent variables distribution. This part can be taken as a regularizer as that of the traditional autoencoder. It forces the encoder's distribution $Q(Z \mid X_i)$ go as close to the latent variables distribution $P(Z)$ as possible by minimizing KL divergence of them. In other words, if the encoder outputs representations are different from the specified distribution, then the regularizer term will penalize the loss function. Otherwise, the penalty will vanish away:

$$L_{VAE} = -\sum_{i=1}^{N}\left(E_{Z\sim Q(Z\mid X_i)}\left[log\left(P(X_i \mid Z)\right)\right] - KL\left(Q(Z \mid X_i)\|P(Z)\right)\right). \tag{9}$$

The last idea for VAE is the way that how to minimize the loss function of Eq. (9) as working on the neural networks, where the algorithms based on gradient decent are popularly adopted. Comparatively, it is feasible to compute the first term in the Eq. (9) as the expectation indicates the reconstruction difference and we can calculate it by the mean squared error between the output of the encoder and the decoder, as similar to that of the traditional autoencoders. However, it is more difficult to compute the second KL divergence directly as $P(Z)$ and $P(X_i \mid Z)$ are all intractable. Fortunately, An effective solution was proposed by Kingma et al. [36] on the assumption that $Q(Z \mid X_i)$ follows a normal distribution $Q(Z \mid X^i) \sim \mathcal{N}(Z; \theta)$, where $\theta = \{\mu_1, \Sigma_1\}$ and μ_1 and Σ_1 are the parameters of the mean and the variance, respectively. For the simplicity, here we assume $P(Z) = \mathcal{N}(Z; 0, I)$, where I is a unitary diagonal matrix. The advantages of this choice make the computation of the KL divergence manageable. We can compute it in the closed form as:

$$KL\left(Q(Z \mid X_i)\|P(Z)\right) = \frac{1}{2}\left(\log\frac{1}{|\Sigma_1|} - D + tr(\Sigma_1) + (\mu_1)^T(\mu_1)\right). \tag{10}$$

D is a constant value that is only relevant to the dimensionality of the distribution.

Additionally, to train a VAE neural structure, the gradient decent should be focused on when error back propagates through the sampling layers. However, we cannot derivate the loss function over the distribution $Q(Z \mid X_i)$ directly as the distribution is a non-continuous operation and has no gradient. To clarify the problem, suppose we can take the derivation of J_{VAE} respect to $Q(Z \mid X_i)$, then we get the gradient expression as following:

$$\frac{\partial L_{VAE}}{\partial Q} = log\left(P(X_i \mid Z)\right) + log(Q) - log(P(Z)) + const. \tag{11}$$

It is clear that the gradient depends not only on the decoder's distribution $P(X_i \mid Z)$ but also on the encoder's distribution $Q(Z \mid X_i)$. Except for the non-continuity of the encoder's distribution, there is no stochastic unit with the neural network. Kingma et al. [36] presented a method named "reparameterization trick" to solve the problem successfully. Instead of drawing from the encoder's representations directly, sampling unit generates μ and σ at first by sampling from the input X. Given $\mu(X)$ and $\sigma(X)$, we can do sampling from $\mathcal{N}(\mu(X), \sigma^2(X))$, and then compute $Z = \mu(X) + \sigma(X) * \varepsilon$, where $\varepsilon \sim \mathcal{N}(0, I)$. Consequently, given a fixed X and ε, L_{VAE} becomes continuous and deterministic for P and Q, which means that derivation of L_{VAE} over Q is computable. Then those algorithms based on the gradient descent (GD) can be effective on VAE neural networks. Comparing to the time-consuming Gibbs sampling methods, algorithms based on GD are much more effective and efficient.

4. ECG preprocessing and enhancement

In this section, we introduce our method on ECG preprocessing and enhancement. The task in this procedure is to split the ECG waves into segments according to the cardiac cycle [28] and then take them as data points for training our models. As described in Section 1, QRS complex is responsible for the activities of ventricular depolarization and repolarization, it has morphologically higher amplitude and sharper peak than other components such as P-wave and T-wave. Therefore, it is much more convenient to detect and locate Q peaks (or R, S peaks) than any other components in these ECG segments. Algorithm 1 describes the procedure of how to split ECG waveforms in detail. The templates selected in algorithm 1 are produced by the contours of the most ECG R wave peaks.

The critical step in Algorithm 1 is how to evaluate the similarity between the selected area on the ECG waveform and the given template. Generally, the mean squared error (MSE) is usually adopted in some ECG recognizing applications. However, the main disadvantage of this method is that it is time-consuming to align the selected area with the given template. For example, there are two pictures with the same curve, the similar value of the pictures may be definitely tiny if the template aligns extremely well or a very large as they do not cover each other at all. Another reasonable approach named the correlation coefficient is being currently used [21, 26]. Instead of computing directly the difference between the ECG waveform and the template as the MSE method, it solves an optimal problem that minimizes the sum of the squares of the offsets of the selected ECG data points to the corresponding points on the template.

We introduce a parameter $hstep$ for the length of the segment of ECG waveforms. It is important to keep $hstep$ lie in a proper range. Otherwise, there are more than one R peaks or none in the segment when the $hstep$ is out of the range. To avoid the awkward situations, there is a trick that let the $hstep$ be proportional to the distance between two adjacent peaks and rather less than it, that is, $hstep \le \frac{\text{sampling rate}}{\text{heart rate}}$. For instance, suppose sampling rate is 250 Hz and heart rate equals 75 times per minute, then $hstep \le 200$. As the heart rate is not a constant during the sampling procedure, then distance can be calculated by the inequation. For this reason, in all of our experiments, the distance is set empirically as the average of that of previous three cardiac periods. The searching step can be initialized as a constant value as there are no any variations on the vertical directions. We keep the $vstep$ equaling 1 in this chapter.

Algorithm 1. ECG R wave peak location algorithm.

input: ECG data file name ***pa***
initial: set segment length ***hstep*** and searching step ***vstep***, empty ECG data buffer ***ecg_v[M]*** and R wave peaks array ***ecg_pos[m]***;
read ECG data into ECG data buffer ***ecg_v*** from ECG data file ***ecg_data_file***;
calculate segment number $N = \lceil L/hstep \rceil$ where L =length(*ecg_v*);
for each segment ***s*** in ***N***
    let search range in vertical direction equal start position;
        while not ***bfind*** **and** ***tp*** > 0 **and** ***bp*** > 0 **do**
            Look for R wave peak in small area of [***rp lp***] in range of [***tp, bp***] using template;
            if ***isfindpeak***() // to decide whether find the target.
                Save the result to ***ecg_pos***;
                break;
            else
                Update range of [***tp, bp***] for next iteration;
            end if
        end while
    update ***rp*** and ***lp*** respectively;
end for
return ECG data array v, R wave peak array ***ecg_pos***;

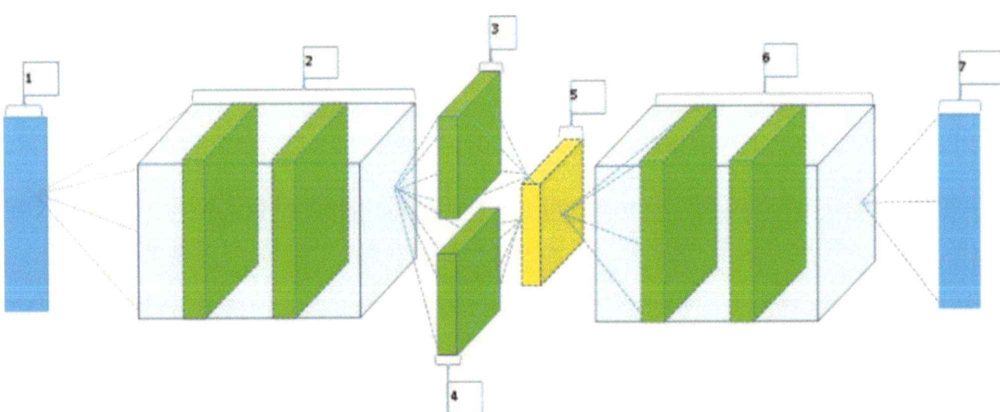

Figure 2. Neural network structure of VAE. It consists of three parts: The encoder, the decoder, and the sampling unit. The encoder (indicating by number 2) and the decoder (indicating by number 6) are all fully connected multilayers neural networks. The sampling unit consists of the mean generator (indicating by number 3), the standard deviation generator (indicating by number 4), and the latent vector generator (indicating by number 5). The structure of the sampling unit lies on the assumption of $Z \backsim N(\mu, \sigma^2)$.

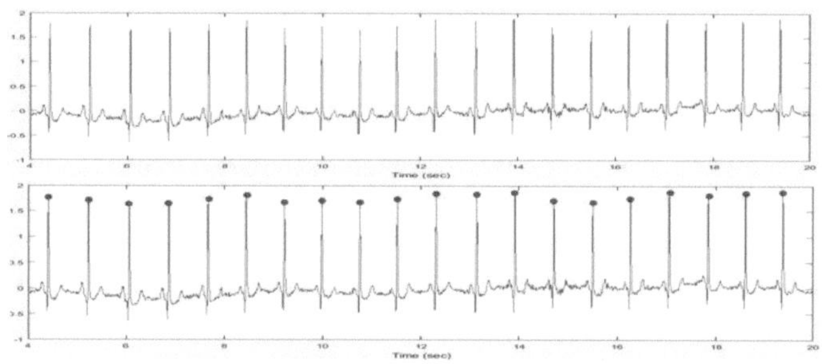

Figure 3. ECG waveform and R-wave peak location adopted from AHA database (top). The bottom picture shows the result of R peaks detection and location for the ECG waveform in the top picture.

Figure 3 shows ECG waveform (top picture) and the R wave peak detection and location (bottom picture). The ECG data are adopted from the American Heart Association (AHA) database on physionnet website [24], which consisted of 80 two-channel ECG recordings and digitized at 250 Hz with 12-bit resolution over a 10-mV range. The recordings in the database are divided into eight classes according to the highest level of ventricular ectopy present.

5. Experimental results and discussion

In this section, we evaluate the performance of VAE and other autoencoder variants described in Section 2.

5.1. ECG signals for multi-classification

To demonstrate the performance of our models on dealing with ECG signals, it is necessary to abstract an intact ECG signal in a cardiac period, which consists of features such as P-wave, QRS complex, and T-wave as described in Section 4. Then detection and location of P-wave becomes more critical step as every cardiac period of ECG signal starts at P-wave. However, as the amplitude of P-wave is smaller than that of QRS complex, and there are many kinds of noise on ECG singles. These factors enlarge the difficulties of abstraction of ECG signals in a cardiac period.

Our solution to alleviate this problem is offered by the fact that it is more feasible to locate R-peaks than to locate the start position of a P-wave. Instead of focusing on the cardiac period, we separate one cardiac period into two semi-cardiac periods at R-peak and then take two parts of the adjacent ECG signals together to form a new period ECG signal, which consists of the second part of the previous cardiac period and the first part of the next one. **Figure 4(a)** shows an example of an ECG signal that is composed of two parts of the adjacent semi-period. Additionally, in the view of information, there is no any feature lost in this separation.

The original ECG recording from ECG database contains several hours of ECG data, and it is unfeasible to train our models using these original ECG data directly. To train our models well, 30,000 ECG signals are abstracted completely from three different ECG databases.

The AHA ECG database, the APNEA ECG database [24], and CHFDB ECG database [24]. Additionally, for ECG data augmentation [32], these ECG data are divided into three different groups according to their source databases and each group has 10,000 ECG signals. On this basis, we augment the ECG data by zeroing a small segment on ECG signals and different positions we selected to zero correspond to different class labels. **Figure 4(b)–(d)** are three examples of our augmentation. Concretely, the labels of **Figure 4(b)–(d)** are 3, 4, and 5, respectively. (We use numbers 1–8 as eight labels for different class of ECG signals in all of our experiments. We add labels for the different classes of ECG signals, not for training our models but for simplifying evaluating the accuracy of our models in testing process.)

To evaluate the properties of our models on denoising for ECG signals, different type noise on different level are added into the original ECG records. These noise include Gaussian noise, salt and pepper noise, and Poisson noise. Moreover, to imitate baseline wandering noise, different amplitude sinusoidal signals are superimposed on the original ECG signals. The coefficients of the sinusoidal signal are 0.01, 0.05, and 0.1, respectively in all of our experiments. **Figure 5** shows the ECG signals polluted by different noises. **Figure 5(a)** and **(c)** show the augmented ECG signals without adding noise except for some one polluted during sampling. **Figure 5(b)** shows ECG signal polluted by the sinusoidal noise and the Gaussian noise. The coefficients for the sinusoidal and for the Gaussian are all 0.01. Nevertheless, the coefficients for the sinusoidal and for the Gaussian are 0.05 and 1 as shown in **Figure 5(d)**. The mean and variance of the Gaussian noise are 0 and 0.01, respectively.

5.2. Recognization of ECG signals

After ECG signals have been abstracted completely by the methods described in Section 5.1, they are used to train VAE model. To compare the effect of the complexity of ECG data on our model, all ECG data are divided into two groups. The first one contains only two classes of ECG records, normal or abnormal. (We call this group as BI dataset) The normal ECG records mean those ones that contain all normal features as shown in **Figures 4** and **5**. The abnormal ECG records in BI dataset contain at least one abnormal feature such as prolonged PR interval, enlarged P-wave, and absence of T-wave. The second group contains 8 classes of ECG records, each of them are produced by zeroing a small segment of ECG

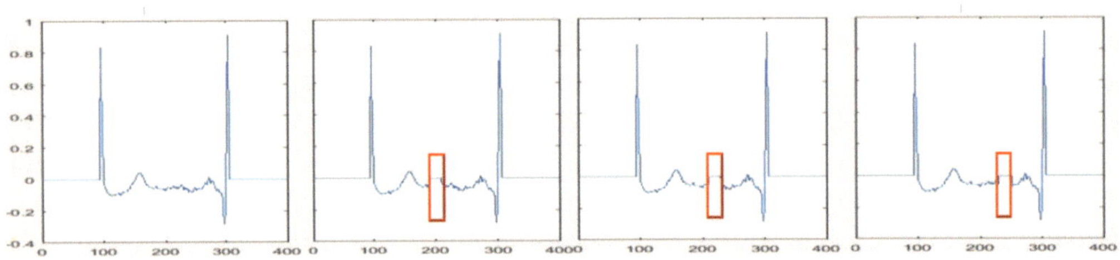

Figure 4. An example of ECG signals that is composed by two parts of the adjacent semi-period. (a) Single period ECG signal between the adjacent R peaks derived by algorithm 1. (b)–(d) are different class ECG signals derived by making a small segment of the same ECG signal zero on different position. The difference is marked by red rectangle area.

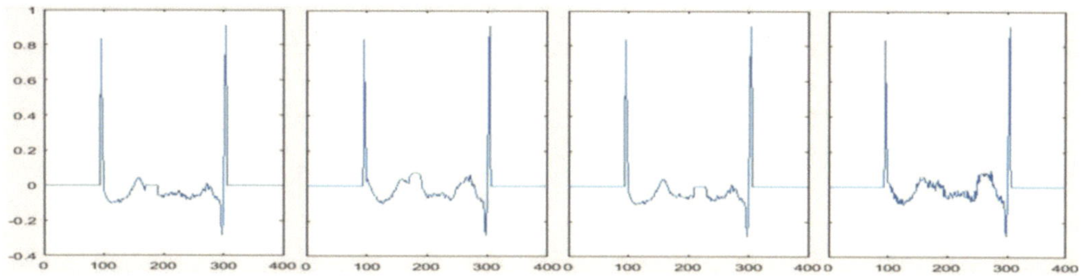

Figure 5. Single periodic ECG signal polluted by different noises. (a) Original ECG signal without adding noise. (b) ECG signal of (a) with Gaussian noise. (c) Original ECG signal with a segment- flatness. (d) ECG signal of (c) contaminated by Gaussian and sine wave noise imitating basing line wander.

data as described in Section 5.1 (We call this group as MI dataset). In order to verify the performance of the VAE model on ECG signals, the parameters of the model are shown in the **Table 1**. **Table 2** shows the performance of the VAE model on recognizing these ECG signals from both BI and MI datasets. The results clearly show that the accuracies of recognition are higher than 95% for MI recorders and even more than 97% for BI recorders. In the view of the data complexity, the result is reasonable because the complexity of MI is much higher than that of BI.

Advantages of VAE model on recognization ECG signals can be further shown by comparasion with other autoecoders such as CAE,DAE, and SAE mentioned in Section 2. In order to make the comparison be fair and reasonable, all of the parameters of the model are the same exept for that of the sampler in VAE model (the values of the parameters can be seen in **Table 1**). Moreover, the ECG records of BI and MI from ahadb database are used to train and test all the models. **Figure 6** shows the accuracy of the models on recognizing the ECG records. Both **(a)** and **(b)** in **Figure 6** take the rate of the representation to the input on size as variable. **Figure 6(a)** takes the BI ECG records from the ahadb as the datasource for the models. Conversely, the MI

Parameter name	Value	Comment
Input size	400	Equal the length of signal
h1	100	First layer of the encoder
h2	10	Second layer of the encoder
z-mean	2	Mean of the sampler
z-variance	2	Variance of sampler
Learning rate	0.01	
Function	Log-sigma	Logarithmic sigma
Optimizer	AdamOptimizer	
Batch size	100	Randomly select samples from the dataset

Table 1. Parameters of VAE model.

DB	Record	ECG no.	Sample no. (10^3)	Class no.	Precision (%)	Error (%)
ahadb	0001	0	10	2	97.70	2.30
ahadb	0001	0	10	8	96.31	3.69
ahadb	0001	1	10	2	96.63	3.37
ahadb	0001	1	10	8	93.91	6.09
ahadb	0201	0	10	2	99.87	0.13
ahadb	0201	0	10	8	96.58	3.42
ahadb	0201	1	10	2	98.10	1.90
ahadb	0201	1	10	8	98.25	1.75
APNEA	a01	0	0.7	2	98.02	1.98
APNEA	a01	0	0.7	8	97.56	2.44
APNEA	a02	0	0.8	2	99.87	0.13
APNEA	a02	0	0.8	8	95.74	4.26
CHFDB	Chf01	0	10	2	99.99	0.01
CHFDB	Chf01	0	10	8	97.65	2.35
CHFDB	Chf01	1	10	2	98.89	1.11
CHFDB	Chf01	1	10	8	96.45	3.55
CHFDB	Chf01	0	10	2	99.75	0.25
CHFDB	Chf01	0	10	8	96.78	3.22
CHFDB	Chf01	1	10	2	99.26	0.74
CHFDB	Chf01	1	10	8	97.92	2.08

Table 2. Performance evaluation of VAE model on three ECG databases.

records from the same dataset are selected in **Figure 6(b)**. It is clear that the accuracy of the VAE model is higher than that of the other models on both BI and MI ECG records, which is at leat 95% on BI records and no more than 90% on MI records. Meanwhile, both figures indicate a fact that the proper rate for the accuracy on the same condition is at 1. The accruy is near 80% when rate falls at 0.5. Simlarly, the accury drops sharply as the rate rise up. Therefore, there is no necessary for representation of ECG signals to compress (rate < 1) or stetch (rate > 1) themselves.

Figure 7 demostrates the performance of the VAE model on denoising for ECG records. The method of adding noise into ECG records in our experiment can be seen in Section 5.1. The coefficient for sinusoidal is 0.05 and the mean and the variance of Gaussian noise are 0 and 0.05, respectively. For the goal of comparison, we take four groups of ECG records (BI, noisy BI, MI and noisy MI) as dataset for the VAE model.

http://dx.doi.org/10.5772/intechopen.76434

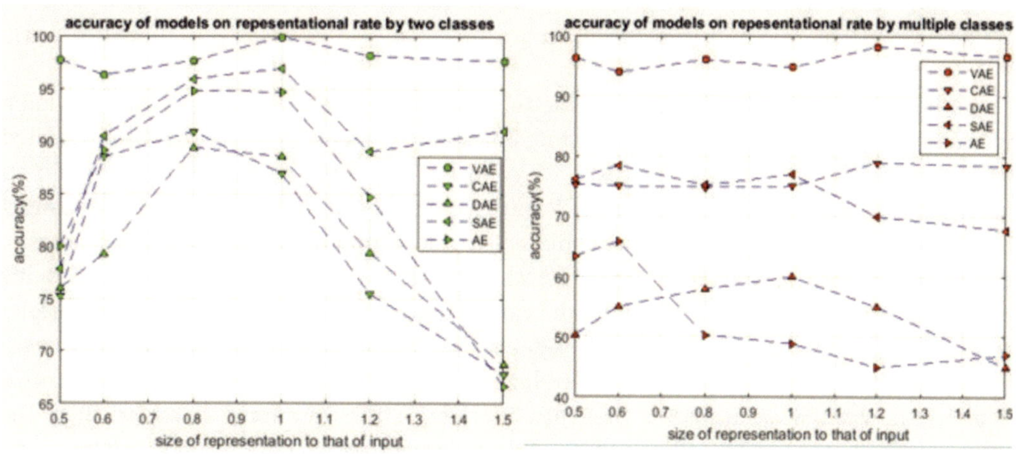

Figure 6. Accuracy of different models on recognition ECG signals from aha database. (a) Accuracy of the models on recognizing ECG signals from BI dataset of ahadb ECG database. (b) Accuracy of the models on recognizing ECG signals from MI dataset of ahadb ECG database.

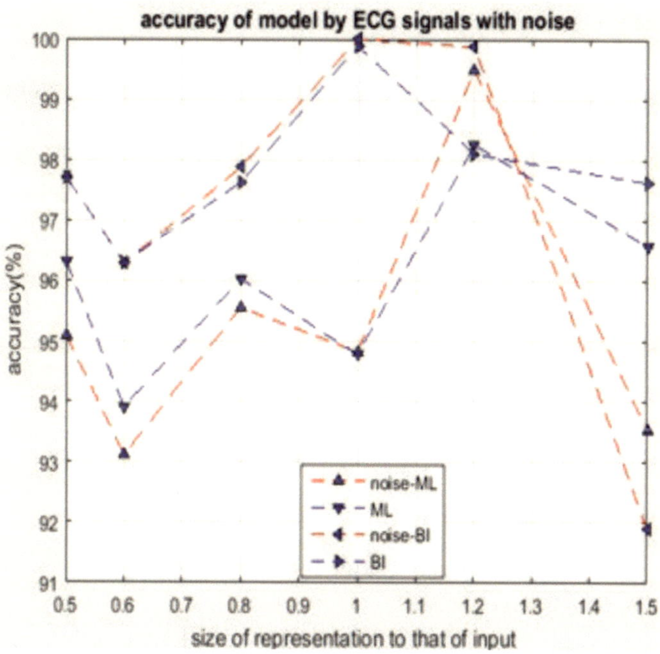

Figure 7. The performance of the VAE model on denoising for ECG records.

The results show that the accuracy under noisy condition is similar to that of without noise on the same dataset. This means that performance of VAE model on ECG recognition is robust to some kinds of noises.

6. Conclusions

In this chapter, we develop a VAE model to recognize a tiny distortion on ECG signals. First, we analyze the characteristics of the features of the ECG signals, which are closely related to ECG components such as P-waves, QRS complex, and T-waves. Second, we explain an algorithm that deals with the location of R peaks. On the basis of the algorithm, we abstract a segment of ECG signal between two adjacent R peaks from three real-life ECG databases. Finally, we train our models by using the selected ECG signals. The results of our experiments demonstrate that the proposed VAE model can be used as an effective tool to automatically recognize ECG signals. Especially, this model is robust to some kinds of noises that are usually produced during the sampling procedures. Furthermore, as a generative model, VAE is a recently established based on the neural networks. The important characteristic of the model is that it can be used in the scenario of the unsupervised learning [31]. Simultaneously, with the emergence of the large amount of unlabeled ECG records and the requirement for real-time diagnosis of heart illness by automatic recognition ECG signals, our method in this chapter can offer a solution to these problems.

In the view of the clinic, future work should put more energy on setting up the set of features of ECG signals, especially, the relationship between the features and the heart diseases. Additionally, because of the physiological characteristics of heart, a single ECG wave may not accurately represent the entire situation of the heart, it is therefore desirable to obtain all of ECG signals from all of 12 or 18 leads. For example, if an anterior wall myocardial infarction happens. Feature of ST-segment elevation reciprocally changes on the ECGs from the leads of I, aVL, and V1–V5. Therefore, the general implementation of VAE model to such clinic situations warrants further study.

Author details

Shaojie Chen[1,2], Zhaopeng Meng[1] and Qing Zhao[2]*

*Address all correspondence to: zhaoqing@tust.edu.cn

1 School of Computer Software, Tianjin University, Tianjin, China

2 School of Computer Science and Informational Engineering, Tianjin University of Science and Technology, Tianjin, China

References

[1] Jordan MI, Ghahramani Z, Jaakkola TS, et al. Introduction to variational methods for graphical models. Machine Learning. 1999;**37**(2):183-233

[2] Bishop, Christopher M. Pattern recognition and machine learning. In: Information Science and Statistics. New York: Springer-Verlag; 2007. p. 049901

[3] Martis RJ, Acharya UR, Min LC. ECG beat classification using PCA, LDA, ICA and discrete wavelet transform. Biomedical Signal Processing and Control. 2013;**8**(5):437-448

[4] Houssein EH, Kilany M, Hassanien AE. Ecg signals classification: A review. International Journal of Medical Engineering and Informatics. 2017;**5**(4):376-396

[5] Banerjee S, Mitra M. Application of cross wavelet transform for ecg pattern analysis and classification. IEEE Transactions on Instrumentation and Measurement. 2014;**63**(2): 326-333

[6] Kærgaard K, Jensen SH, Puthusserypady S. A comprehensive performance analysis of EEMD-BLMS and DWT-NN hybrid algorithms for ECG denoising. Biomedical Signal Processing and Control. 2016;**25**:178-187

[7] Nazarahari M, Namin SG, Markazi AHD, Anaraki AK. A multi-wavelet optimization approach using similarity measures for electrocardiogram signal classification. Biomedical Signal Processing and Control. 2015;**20**:142-151

[8] Rui R, Couto P. A neural network approach to ECG denoising. CoRR, abs/1212.5217,2012

[9] Xiong P, Wang H, Liu M, Zhou S, Hou Z, Liu X. ECG signal enhancement based on improved denoising auto-encoder. Engineering Applications of Artificial Intelligence. 2016;**52**(C):194-202

[10] Xiong P, Wang H, Liu M, Lin F, Hou Z, Liu X. A stacked contractive denoising autoencoder for ECG signal denoising. Physiological Measurement. 2016;**37**(12):2214

[11] Zhou L, Yan Y, Qin X, Yuan C, Que D, Wang L. Deep learning-based classification of massive electrocardiography data. In: Advanced Information Management, Communicates, Electronic and Automation Control Conference; IEEE; 2017. pp. 780-785

[12] Yan Y, Qin X, Wu Y, Zhang N, Fan J, Wang L. A Restricted Boltzmann Machine Based Two-Lead Electrocardiography Classification. In: Wearable and Implantable Body Sensor Networks (BSN), IEEE 12th International Conference on IEEE. 2015 Jun 9. pp. 1-9

[13] Rangayyan, Rangaraj M. Biomedical Signal Analysis: A Case-Study Approach. Piscataway, NJ: IEEE Press, 2002

[14] Qi H, Liu X, Pan C. Discrete Wavelet Soft Threshold Denoise Processing for ECG Signal. In: International Conference on Intelligent Computation Technology and Automation; Vol. 2; IEEE Computer Society; 2010. pp. 126-129

[15] Ziarani AK, Konrad A. A nonlinear adaptive method of elimination of power line interference in ECG signals. IEEE Transactions on Bio-Medical Engineering. 2002;**49**(6):540

[16] Alfaouri M, Daqrouq K. ECG signal denoising by wavelet transform thresholding. American Journal of Applied Sciences. 2008;**5**(3):276-281

[17] Dewangan NK, Kowar MK. A review on ECG signal de-noising, QRS complex, P and T wave detection techniques. International journal of innovative research in electrical, electronics, instrumentation and control engineering. 2015;**3**(2):10-14

[18] El Hanine M, Abdelmounim E, Haddadi R, Belaguid A. Electrocardiogram signal denoising using discrete wavelet transform. In: Technology of Computer: English Edition; Vol. 2; 2014. pp. 98-104

[19] Blanco-Velasco M, Weng B, Barner KE. ECG signal denoising and baseline wander correction based on the empirical mode decomposition. Computers in Biology and Medicine. 2008;**38**(1):1-13

[20] Li N, Li P. An improved algorithm based on EMD-wavelet for ECG signal de-noising. In: International Joint Conference on Computational Sciences and Optimization; Vol. 1; IEEE; 2009. pp. 825-827

[21] Chan HL, Chen GU, Lin MA, Fang SC. Heartbeat detection using energy thresholding and template match. In: International Conference of the Engineering in Medicine and Biology Society, 2005 (IEEE-EMBS 2005); Vol. 6; IEEE; 2006. pp. 6668-6670

[22] Krasteva V, Jekova I. QRS template matching for recognition of ventricular ectopic beats. Annals of Biomedical Engineering. 2007;**35**(12):2065

[23] Zhou Y, Hu X, Tang Z, Ahn AC. Sparse representation-based ECG signal enhancement and QRS detection. Physiological Measurement. 2016;**37**(12):2093

[24] Goldberger AL, Amaral LAN, Glass L, Hausdorff JM, Ivanov PC, Mark RG, et al. Physiobank, physiotoolkit, and physionet components of a new research resource for complex physiologic signals. Circulation. 2000;**101**(23):E215

[25] Chiu C-C, Lin T-H, Liau B-Y. Using correlation coefficient in ECG waveform for arrhythmia detection. Biomedical Engineering Applications Basis & Communications. 2005;**17** (03):0500023

[26] Rifai S, Vincent P, Muller X, Glorot X, Bengio Y. Contractive auto-encoders: Explicit invariance during feature extraction. In: Proceedings of the 28th International Conference on International Conference on Machine Learning. Omnipress: 2011 Jun 28. pp. 833-840

[27] Vincent P, Larochelle H, Bengio Y, Manzagol PA. Extracting and composing robust features with denoising autoencoders. In: International Conference on Machine Learning; ACM; 2008. pp. 1096-1103

[28] Liu G, Luan Y. An adaptive integrated algorithm for noninvasive fetal ECG separation and noise reduction based on ICA-EEMD-WS. Medical & Biological Engineering & Computing. 2015;**53**(11):1113

[29] Rahhal MMA, Bazi Y, Alhichri H, Alajlan N, Melgani F, Yager RR. Deep learning approach for active classification of electrocardiogram signals. Information Sciences. 2016;**345**(C): 340-354

[30] Vincent P, Larochelle H, Lajoie I, Bengio Y, Manzagol PA. Stacked denoising autoencoders: Learning useful representations in a deep network with a local denoising criterion. Journal of Machine Learning Research. 2010;**11**(12):3371-3408

[31] Min S, Lee B, Yoon S. Deep learning in bioinformatics. Briefings in Bioinformatics. 2016;**18**(5):851

[32] Bouthillier X, Konda K, Vincent P, Memisevic R. Dropout as data augmentation. arXiv preprint arXiv:1506.08700. 2015 Jun 29

[33] Carbonetto P, Stephens M. Scalable variational inference for bayesian variable selection in regression, and its accuracy in genetic association studies. Bayesian Analysis. 2012; **7**(1):73-107

[34] Challis E, Barber D. Gaussian Kullback-Leibler Approximate Inference. 2013. Available from: JMLR.org

[35] Foti NJ, Xu J, Laird D, Fox EB. Stochastic variational inference for hidden Markov models. In: International Conference on Neural Information Processing Systems; Vol. 4; MIT Press; 2014. pp. 3599-3607

[36] Kingma DP, Welling M. Auto-Encoding Variational Bayes. New York: Springer-Verlag; 2013

[37] Blei DM, Kucukelbir A, Mcauliffe JD. Variational inference: A review for statisticians. Journal of the American Statistical Association. 2017;**112**(518):859-877

Chapter 6

A Survey on Methods of Image Processing and Recognition for Personal Identification

Ryszard S. Choras

Additional information is available at the end of the chapter

http://dx.doi.org/10.5772/intechopen.76116

Abstract

The network of blood vessels possesses several properties that make a good biometric feature for personal identification: (1) they are difficult to damage and modify; (2) they are difficult to simulate using a fake template; and (3) vein information can represent the liveness of the person. In the process of recognition of the network of blood vessels, we encounter two main difficulties: the first difficulty concerns the enhancement of the image of blood vessels obtained from the camera working in visible and/or infrared light, and the second one concerns the process of extraction of features and methods of classification. In the first part, this chapter presents the basic methods of preprocessing biometric images. In the second part, we discuss the process of feature extraction with particular emphasis on the feature extraction from images depicting the network of blood vessels. This applies to texture analysis using the co-occurrence matrix, Gabor filtration, moments, and topological features using cross points. In the third part, we present the methods of processing images of the blood vessel network of dorsal part of the hand and wrist. We also discuss the process of reducing the dimensionality of a feature vector using the principal components analysis method.

The results of the recognition of the network of blood vessel patterns show the suitability of the method for biometric identification purposes.

Keywords: biometrics, vein patterns, feature extraction, co-occurrence matrix, Gabor's filters, classification

1. Introduction

Biometrics is a powerful field of science for identifying a person using their physiological and behavioral features [1, 2]. Biometrics is the automatic recognition of people based on behavioral or physiological characteristics. During recognition given users are assigned to prescribed classes. We extract the essential features of the object and use these features to classify the object.

Biometric systems in general perform two tasks: identification and verification (recognition) of people (**Figure 1**). The process of verification (recognition) boils down to distinguishing a specific person from a limited number of people whose biometric data are known. The identification consists of determining the vector of features corresponding to the person being subjected to the identification process and trying to find a match between this vector and the feature vectors in the database containing records (feature vectors) concerning people. As a result, we get a list of the most similar individuals in the database. Identification is much more difficult [3, 4].

Images play an important role in the identification process of people. Image processing and recognition are fields that use complex signal and image processing algorithms.

The image in digital form is stored as a two-dimensional array. Formally

$$D = \{(x, y) | x \epsilon M, y \epsilon N\} \tag{1}$$

and

$$F = \{f(x, y) | (x, y) \epsilon D \text{ and } f(x, y) \epsilon\, 0, 1, \cdots, G - 1\} \tag{2}$$

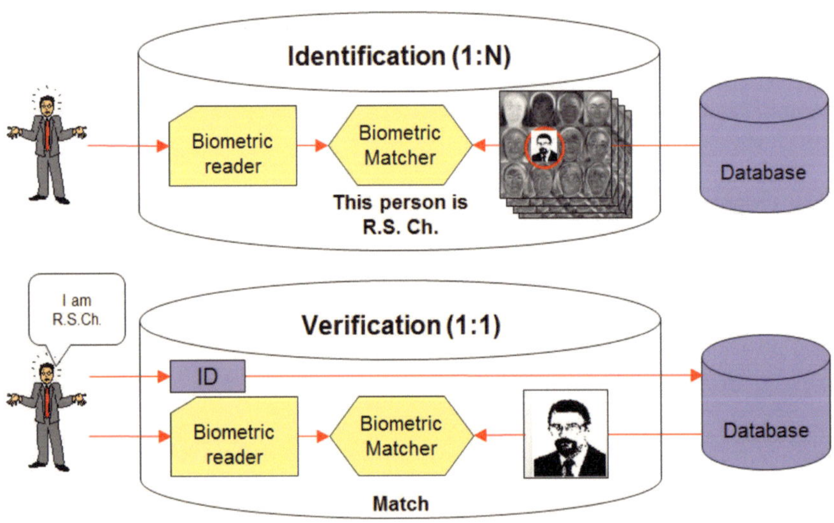

Figure 1. Identification and verification process.

where $= \{1, 2, \cdots, m\}$, $N = \{1, 2, \cdots, n\}$, and *G-1* is the gray/color maximum value of each resolution cell.

The components of an image processing system are presented on **Figure 2**.

The processing generally comprises the steps of acquiring an image, selecting the desired color space, improving image quality, image segmentation, and features extraction for the recognition. Recognition process involves several stages—extraction features and dimensionality reduction which selects the best set of features and rejects irrelevance. The resultant feature vector is the basis for classification.

The image is usually obtained using a CCD camera or NIR camera. It can be a color image (three-color components) or a grayscale image. Usually, color space (RGB with 24 bit) is converted to gray color space (8 bit).

Below, some steps shown in image processing system on **Figure 2** will be explained in more detail [5].

Image processing operations can be divided into (**Figure 3**):

- Processing of single points of the image.
- Operations that use pixel group processing.

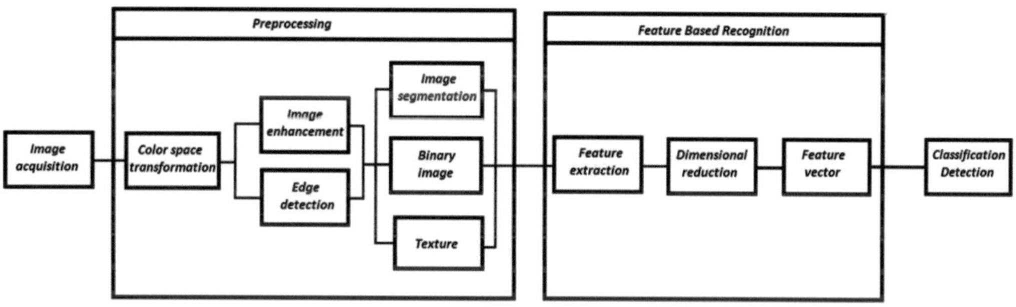

Figure 2. Schematic diagram of the image processing and recognition system for personal identification.

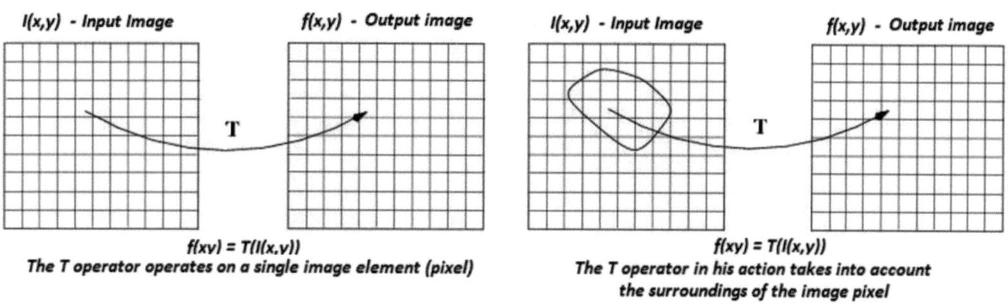

Figure 3. Image processing operations.

The first group includes operations related to modification histogram, while the second group includes operations related to edge detection and various types of image filtration.

Transforming the brightness scale of image elements enables:

- In the case where the brightness range does not cover the entire scale available for the image, the extension of the range (the effect of increase contrast)
- Emphasizing certain brightness ranges and suppressing others
- Modifying the brightness of image elements to obtain a uniform image frequency of the occurrence of appropriate levels of brightness

In practice, transformation T can be a logarithmic transformation, exponential transformation, etc. (**Figure 4**).

If h_g represents the number of pixels in an image with intensity g, e.g., $f(x, y) = g$, then the probability density function is defined as $prob(f(x, y) = g = \frac{h_g}{MN}$ for $g = 0, 1, \cdots, G-1$, and the cumulative density function is defined as $c(f(x, y) = g) = \sum_{g=0}^{G-1} prob(f(x, y) = g$ for $g = 0,$ $1, \cdots, G-1$.

The gray levels are modified as [5, 6]

$$\overline{g} = (\max - \min)\cdot c(f(x, y) = g) + \min \tag{3}$$

where max and min are, respectively, the maximum and minimum values of image gray level [6] (**Figures 5** and **6**).

One of the methods of noise elimination ("salt pepper" type) and other image distortions is median filtering (MF). Median filtering is a nonlinear operation, and this fact complicates the mathematical analysis of its properties. It is implemented by moving the window (the mask) along the lines of the digital image and changing the value of the middle window element by

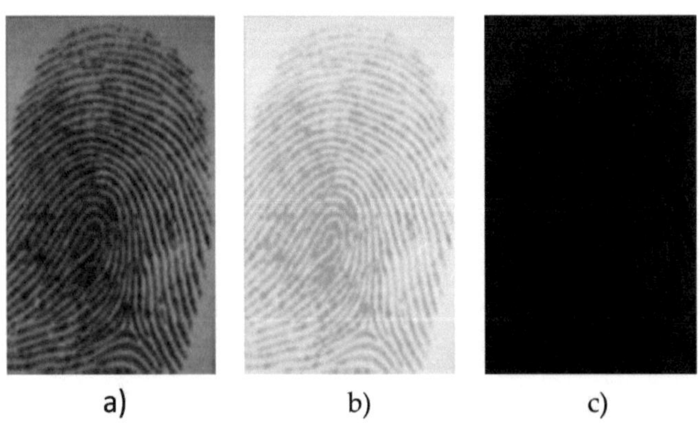

Figure 4. The original fingerprint image (a), the result of logarithmic transformation (b), and the exponential transformation (c).

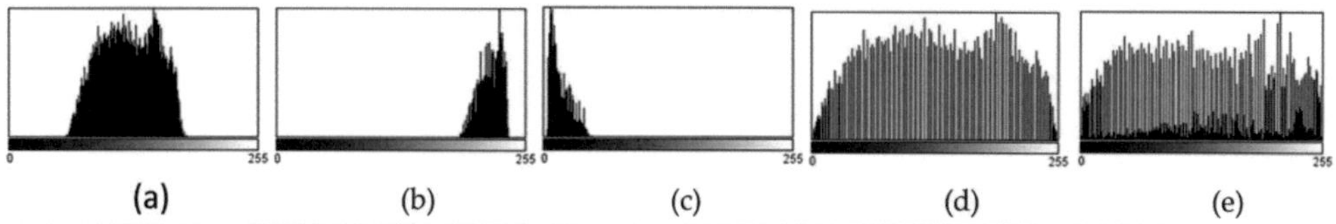

Figure 5. Histogram of the original fingerprint image (a) and histogram-enhanced images after logarithmic transformation (b), exponential transformation (c), equalization (d), and CLAHE (contrast limited adaptive histogram equalization) (e).

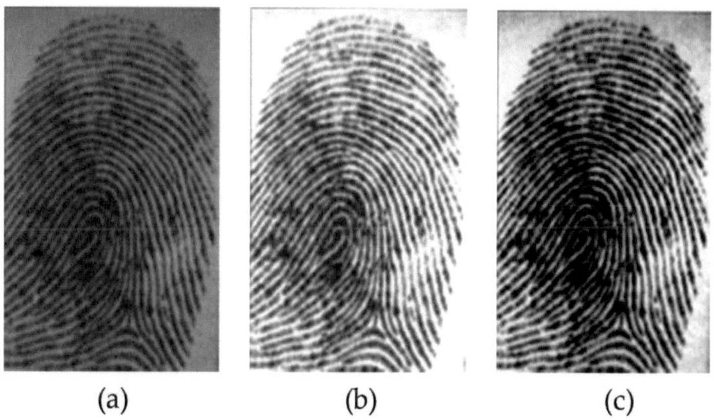

Figure 6. The original fingerprint image (a), enhanced image (b), and stretched image (c).

the median value of the elements inside the window. MF allows you to keep sharp changes in brightness and high efficiency in eliminating impulsive noise [5].

The 2D *MF* for an image $f(x, y)$ is defined as

$$\widehat{f}(x, y) = median_{A_1} f(x, y) = median[f(x + r, y + s)] \tag{4}$$

where A_1 is the *MF* window.

MF allows you to keep sharp changes in brightness and high efficiency in eliminating impulsive noise (**Figure 7**).

Edges carry useful information about object boundaries which can be used for further analysis. Edge detectors can be grouped into two classes: (a) local techniques which use operators on local image neighborhoods and (b) global techniques.

Gradient estimates is done as

$$\widehat{f} = \left[(f_x)^2 + \left(f_y\right)^2 \right]^{\frac{1}{2}} \tag{5}$$

and can be expressed by (**Table 1**)

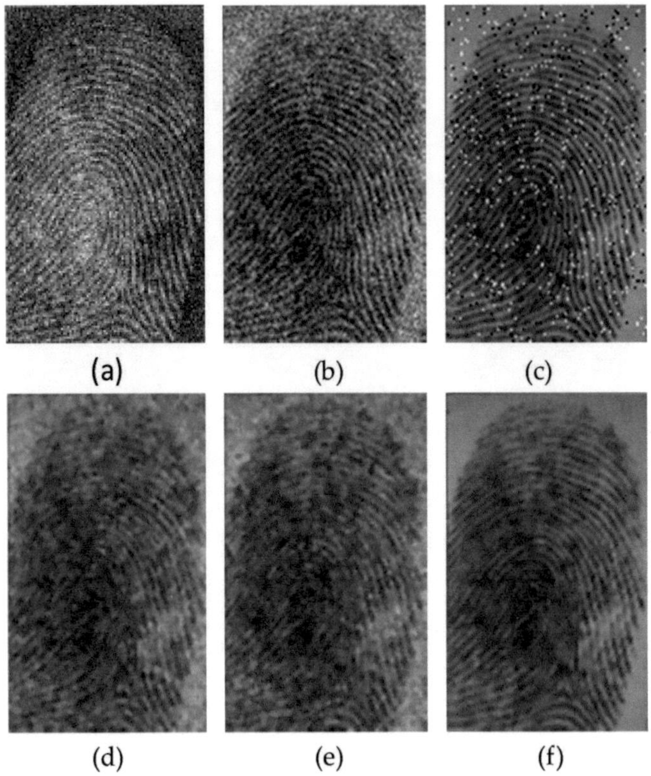

Figure 7. Median filtration: Original image (a), image with noise (b), image with "salt and pepper" noise; (d), (e), and (f) image after MF.

$$\widehat{f} = \left[\left(w_1^t f^4 \right)^2 + \left(w_2^t f^4 \right)^2 \right]^{\frac{1}{2}} \tag{6}$$

or

$$\widehat{f} = \left[\left(w_1^t f^8 \right)^2 + \left(w_2^t f^8 \right)^2 \right]^{\frac{1}{2}} \tag{7}$$

where f^4 and f^8 are neighborhood pixels.

Another popular operator, not shown in **Table 1**, is the Canny edge detector operator implemented in accordance with the **Figure 8** [7].

Examples of applications of edge detection operators are shown in **Figure 9**.

Let $f(x, y)$ be a function of the brightness of the analyzed image; X a finite subset of the plane on which the function $f(x, y)$ is specified; $S = \{S_1, S_2, \cdots, S_K\}$ the division of X into K non–empty subsets $S_i, i = 1, 2, \cdots, K,$ and *Reg* the rule specified on the set S and assuming the value *true* if and only if any pair of points from each subset S_i corresponds to a certain homogeneity criterion.

http://dx.doi.org/10.5772/intechopen.76116

Edge detector operators	Partial derivatives along x and y axes	Weight vectors	Kernels
Differential	$f_x = [(x,y)f - f(x,y+1)] - [f(x+1,y) - f(x+1,y+1)]$ $f_y = [f(x+1,y) - f(x,y)] - [f(x+1,y+1) - f(x,y+1)]$	$w_1 = \begin{bmatrix} 1 \\ -1 \\ 1 \\ -1 \end{bmatrix}; w_2 = \begin{bmatrix} -1 \\ -1 \\ 1 \\ 1 \end{bmatrix}$	2×2
Roberts edge detectors	$f_x = f(x,y) - f(x+1,y+1)$ $f_y = f(x+1,y) - f(x,y+1)$	$w_1 = \begin{bmatrix} 1 \\ 0 \\ 0 \\ -1 \end{bmatrix}; w_2 = \begin{bmatrix} 0 \\ -1 \\ 1 \\ 0 \end{bmatrix}$	2×2
Max. difference	$f_x = \max(f(x,y), f(x+1,y)f(x,y+1), f(x+1,y+1))$ $f_x = -\min(f(x,y), f(x+1,y)f(x,y+1), f(x+1,y+1)f(x+1,y+1))$	there is no	2×2
Prewitt edge detector	$f_x = (f(x-1,y-1) + f(x,y-1) + f(x+1,y-1)) - (f(x-1,y+1) + f(x,y+1) + f(x+1,y+1))$ $f_y = (f(x+1,y-1) + f(x+1,y) + f(x+1,y+1)) - (f(x-1,y-1) + f(x-1,y) + f(x-1,y+1))$	$w_1 = \begin{bmatrix} 1 \\ 0 \\ -1 \\ 1 \\ 0 \\ -1 \\ 1 \\ 0 \\ -1 \end{bmatrix}; w_2 = \begin{bmatrix} -1 \\ -1 \\ -1 \\ 0 \\ 0 \\ 0 \\ 1 \\ 1 \\ 1 \end{bmatrix}$	3×3
Sobel edge detector	$f_x = (f(x-1,y-1) + 2f(x,y-1) + f(x+1,y-1)) - (f(i-1,y+1) + 2f(x,y+1) + f(x+1,y+1))$ $f_y = (f(x+1,y-1) + 2f((x+1,j) + f(x+1,y+1)) - (f(x-1,y-1) + 2f(x-1,y) + f(x-1,y+1))$	$w_1 = \begin{bmatrix} 1 \\ 0 \\ -1 \\ 2 \\ 0 \\ -2 \\ 1 \\ 0 \\ -1 \end{bmatrix}; w_2 = \begin{bmatrix} -1 \\ -2 \\ -1 \\ 0 \\ 0 \\ 0 \\ 1 \\ 2 \\ 1 \end{bmatrix}$	3×3

Table 1. Differential gradient operators.

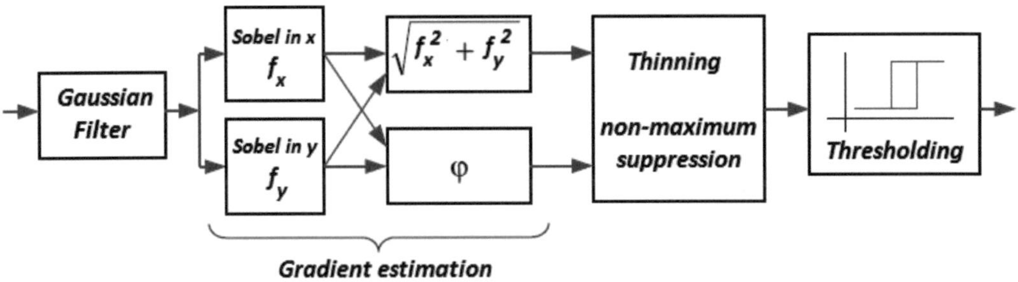

Figure 8. Canny edge detector.

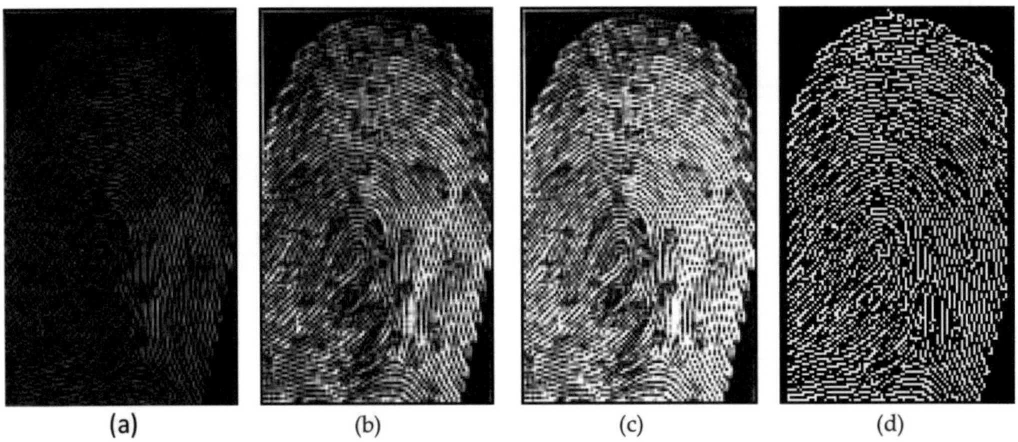

Figure 9. Original image after edge detector operator: Roberts (a), Prewitt (b), Sobel (c), and Canny.

The segmentation of the image $f(x,y)$ according to the *Reg* rule is the division $S = \{S_1, S_2, \cdots, S_K\}$ corresponding to the conditions as follows:

$$\begin{aligned} &\text{a. } \bigcup_{i=1}^{K} S_i = X; \\ &\text{b. } S_i \bigcap S_j = 0, \quad \forall i \neq j; \\ &\text{c. } Reg(S_i) = true \quad \forall i; \\ &\text{d. } Reg(S_i \cap S_j) = false \quad \forall i \neq j. \end{aligned} \tag{8}$$

The *Reg* rule specifies a certain homogeneity criterion and depends on the function of $f(x,y)$. We consider segmentation as

$$Seg : f(x,y) \rightarrow s_{i,j} \tag{9a}$$

$$s_{i,j} = \lambda_i \quad for \quad (x,y) \in S_i, \quad i = 1, 2, \cdots, K \tag{9b}$$

where $f(x,y)$ and $s_{i,j}$ are functions that define the input image and the segmented image, respectively, while λ_i is the label (name) of S_i area.

2. Feature extraction

Methods for feature extraction on biometric traits can be categorized into geometrical analysis and textural analysis (**Table 2**).

The texture image can be seen as an image area containing repetitive pixel intensity patterns arranged in a certain structural manner. The concept of texture has no formal and mathematical definition, but there are a number of methods for extracting texture features that can be roughly divided into model-based (fractal and stochastic method), statistical, and using signal processing algorithms.

Methods using signal processing algorithms (in the frequency domain and/or space-frequency domain) are widely used in transform-based texture analysis, e.g., Fourier transform, Gabor transform, Riesz transform, Radon transform, and wavelet transform.

Biometric physiological modality	Geometrical features	Texture features
Fingerprint	Minutiae singular points Delta points Triangulation methods Crossing number	Analysis texture pattern composed with ridges and valleys Spatial distribution of minutiae points
Palmprint	Principal lines. Line edge map Wrinkles Palmar friction ridges Shape-oriented features	Local line binary pattern Co-occurrence matrix
Finger knuckle print	Shape-oriented features: lines, curves, contours	Curvelet Co-occurrence matrix Wavelets
Hand geometry	Shape-oriented features Finger length and width	—
Face	Spatial relationship among eyes, lips, nose, chin	Gabor's filtering LBP
Ear	Force field transformation 2D and 3D shape descriptors	Moment invariants
Iris	—	Phase-based method Gabor's filtering
Periocular	Geometry of eyelids, eye folds, eye corners	LBP Histogram of oriented gradients SIFT (shift-invariant feature transform)
Retina	Minutiae singular points Crossing number	Gabor's filtering
Vein Hand vein Finger vein Forearm vein	Bifurcation points Ending points	Gabor's filtering Riesz transform Wavelet, curvelet Radon transform

Table 2. Biometric feature extraction methods.

One of the popular representations of texture feature is the co-occurrence matrix proposed by Haralick et al. [8–10]. The gray-level co-occurrence matrix (GLCM) $C_d(k,l)$ counts the co – occurrence of pixels with gray values *k* and *l* at a given distance *d* and then extracts statistical measures from this matrix. The element of co-occurrence matrix is defined as

$$c(k,l) = \sum_{\substack{x,y\in D \\ (x+s,y+t)\in D}} \begin{cases} 1 \ if \ (f(x,y) = k \ and \ f(x+\Delta x, y+\Delta y) = l \\ 0 \qquad otherwise \end{cases} + \sum_{\substack{x,y\in D \\ (x+s,y+t)\in D}} \begin{cases} 1 \ if \ (f(x,y) = l \ and \ f(x+\Delta x, y+\Delta y) = k \\ 0 \qquad otherwise \end{cases} \tag{10}$$

These features provide information about the texture and are as follows:

$$\begin{aligned} &\text{Element difference moment of order p}: \sum_k\sum_l (k-l)^p C_d(k,l). \ \text{When p} = 2, \text{it} \\ &\text{is called the contrast;} \\ &\text{Entropy.Entropy} = -\sum_k\sum_l C_d(k,l)\log C_d(k,l); \\ &\text{Energy.Energy} = \sum_k\sum_l C_d(k,l)^2; \\ &\text{Inverse difference moment.IDM} = \sum_k\sum_l \frac{1}{1+(k-l)^2} C_d(k,l). \\ &\text{Correlation.Corr} = \frac{\sum_k\sum_l (k,l)C_d(k,l) - \mu_x\mu_y}{\sigma_x\sigma_y}. \end{aligned} \tag{11}$$

The distance *d* is most often represented in polar coordinates in the form of a discrete distance and an orientation angle. In practice, we use four angles, namely, $0^{\circ}, 45^{\circ}, 90^{\circ}, 135^{\circ}$ (**Figure 10**).

Mathematically, Gabor filters is defined as [11]

$$Gab_{\omega,\theta}(x,y) = \frac{1}{2\pi\sigma_x\sigma_y}\exp\left\{-\left(\frac{(x\cos\theta + y\sin\theta)^2}{2\sigma_x^2} + \frac{(-x\sin\theta + y\cos\theta)^2}{2\sigma_y^2}\right)\right\} \left[exp\left\{i(\omega x\cos\theta + \omega y\sin\theta)\right\} - exp\left\{-\frac{\omega^2\sigma^2}{2}\right\}\right] \tag{12}$$

Typically, Gabor's filter bank was created by varying the frequency parameter, the orientation parameter, and the variance parameter (**Figure 11**).

Gabor's features are obtained by convolution of the image *f (x, y)* with the $Gab_{\omega,\theta}(x,y)$ filter:

$$G_{\omega,\theta}(x,y) = f(x,y) * Gab_{\omega,\theta}(x,y) \tag{13}$$

where $*$ is the convolution operator [11–13].

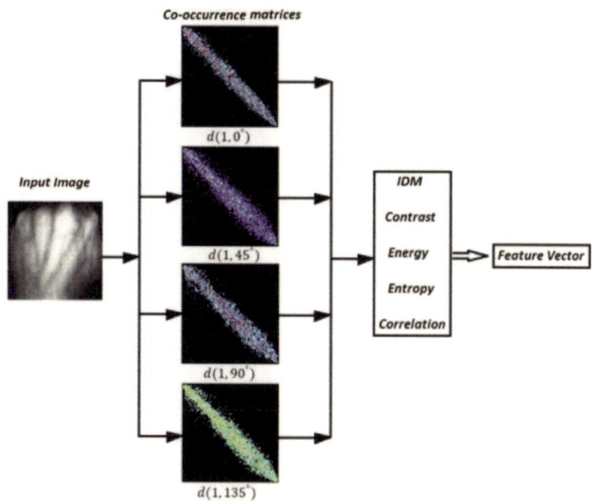

Figure 10. The gray-level co-occurrence matrices.

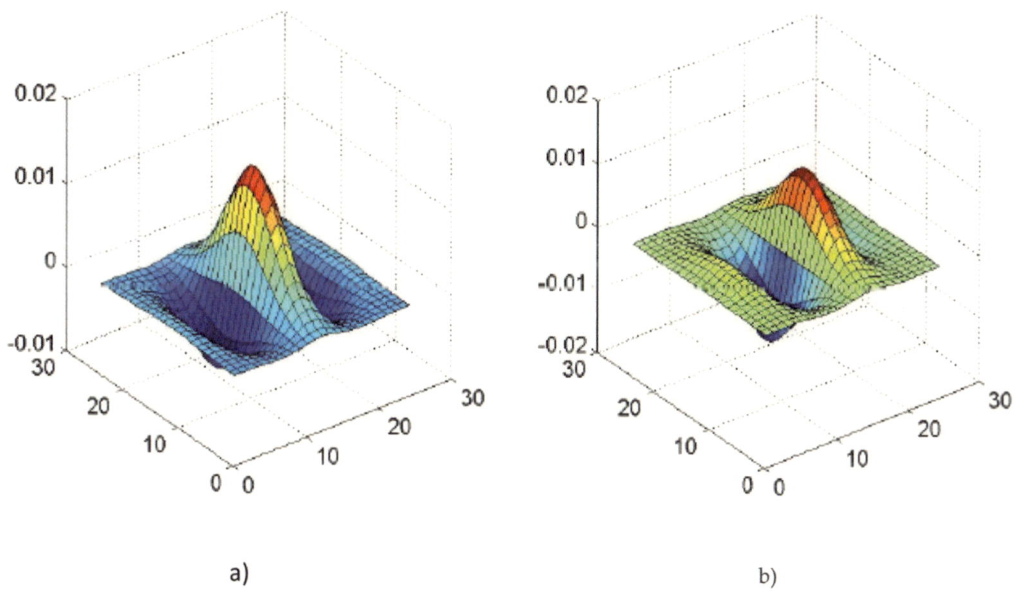

Figure 11. 2D Gabor's filters in spatial domain: (a) real and (b) imaginary components.

Moment-based features can be successfully used as elements of a feature vector in biometrics using blood vessel network [13, 14].

The geometric moments of order $(p+q)$ of the image $f(x,y)$ is determined by

$$m_{pq} = \sum_{x}\sum_{y} f(x,y)\, h_{pq}(x,y) \tag{14}$$

where $h_{pq}(x,y)$ is a certain polynomial in which x is the degree p, while y is the degree q. If $h_{pq}(x,y) = x^p y^q$, then we consider the geometrical moments of the image (x,y).

Infinite set of moments $\{m_{pq},\ \ p,q = 0,1,\cdots\}$ uniquely specifies $f(x,y)$ and vice versa.

Central moments are defined by

$$\mu_{pq} = \sum_x \sum_y (x-\overline{x})^p\ (y-\overline{y})^q f(x,y) \tag{15}$$

where $\overline{x} = \frac{m_{10}}{m_{00}}, \overline{y} = \frac{m_{01}}{m_{00}}$.

Standardized central moments receiving as

$$\eta_{pq} = \frac{\mu_{pq}}{\mu_{00}^{\gamma}} \tag{16}$$

where $\gamma = \frac{1}{2}\ \ (p+q)+1,\ \ dla\ p+q = 2,3,\cdots$.

We usually use the first seven combinations of central moments of order 3 known in the literature as Hu moments [15].

The basic set of geometrical moments is non-orthogonal which makes selection of features difficult.

Zernike's moments are orthogonal and invariant to rotation, translation, and scale change. The complex set of Zernike's moments is determined by [16]

$$A_{nm} = \frac{n+1}{\pi} \sum_{x=1}^{M} \sum_{y=1}^{N} Z_{nm}^{*}(\rho,\theta) f(x,y) \tag{17}$$

where $Z_{nm}(\rho,\theta) = R_{nm}(\rho)e^{jm\theta}$ and $R_{nm}(\rho) = \sum_{s=0}^{\frac{(n-|m|)}{2}} \frac{(-1)^s\ [(n-s)!]\ \rho^{n-2s}}{s!\left(\frac{n+|m|}{2}-s\right)!\left(\frac{n-|m|}{2}-s\right)!}$.

When calculating Zernike's moments, the size of the image determines the disk size, and the disk center is taken as the origin. In the case of considering moments on the order of 7, we get 20 Zernike's moments.

In the case of biometric data using images of retinal blood vessels and conjunctival blood vessels, one of the stages of creating a vector of features is to determine geometrical features based on the topological properties of the image [5, 17].

The number of connected points around the point f_0 is determined by

$$N_c^4 = \sum_{k \in S} \left(f_k - f_k f_{k+1} f_{k+2}\right) \tag{18}$$

where 4 denote the four-element neighborhood of the image point, f_k assumes the value 0 or 1, and S denotes the set of integers [17]. In the case where $k \geq 9$, its value is defined as $k-8$.

If $N_c^4 = 3, f_k$ is the bifurcation point, and if $N_c^4 = 4, f_{k'}$ is the cross point.

The feature vector defining the topology of blood vessels is made up of the number of bifurcation points, number of crossing points, coordinates of bifurcation points, and coordinates of crossing points.

By using the relationship between the characteristic points of the user blood vessel image and blood vessel image of template, we can calculate the matching score results.

3. Vein biometrics: feature extraction from hand dorsal and wrist images

One of the most promising and intensively developed biometric methods is the method using the network of blood vessels. The pattern of blood vessels is unique for every human being and also in the case of twins. It is also stable over time [18]. Biometrics associated with the network of blood vessels has a significant advantage over other biometric methods, namely [1, 4, 18]:

- Allows only identification of living people: the NIR camera records the image only in the case of deoxygenated hemoglobin, and this is possible only in the living organism [19, 26];
- The network of blood vessels is inside the body, and it is practically impossible to reproduce outside of it, which results in very high level of safety.
- Usually, we use the network of blood vessels associated with the following parts of the body:
- Eye. This applies first of all not only to the retinal blood vessels but also to the blood vessels of the conjunctiva.
- Hand. In this case, we are talking about the network of blood vessels of the finger, palm, hand dorsal, wrist, and forearm [20, 24, 25].

Figure 12 Shows the networks of blood vessels used in biometry.

We will consider images from **Figure 12(e)** and **(f)**, which can be obtained in one process of acquiring biometric patterns. In the literature on the subject, the analysis of this type of images for biometrics is referred to as *dorsal vein biometrics* and *wrist vein biometrics* [27, 28].

3.1. Vein biometrics

In the process of identifying people on the basis of dorsal vein images, we use a feature vector constructed from two parts: features calculated on the basis of the co-occurrence matrix and features calculated using Gabor filtration operation [21–23].

We consider the dorsal vein images shown in **Figure 13**.

We analyze the co-occurrence matrix for $= \{(1,0^\circ),(1,45^\circ),(1,90^\circ),(1,135^\circ)\}$. The five features calculated for each value of distance d are shown in **Table 3**.

As a result, on the basis of the co-occurrence matrix, we obtain 40 features.

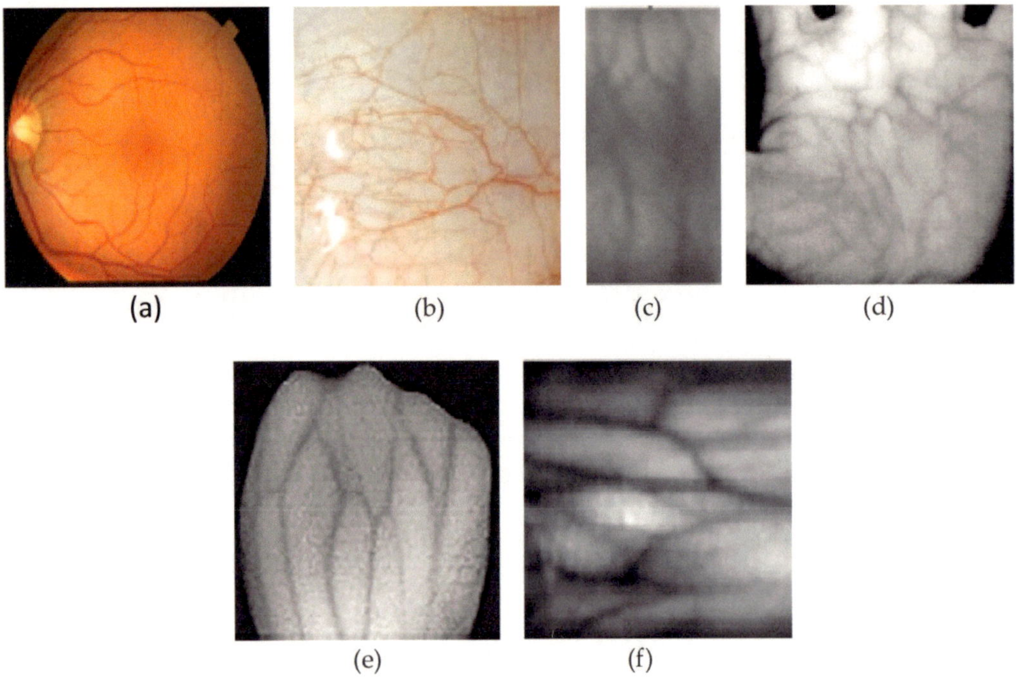

Figure 12. The networks of blood vessels: Retina (a), conjunctiva (b), finger (c), palm (d), hand dorsal (e), and wrist (f).

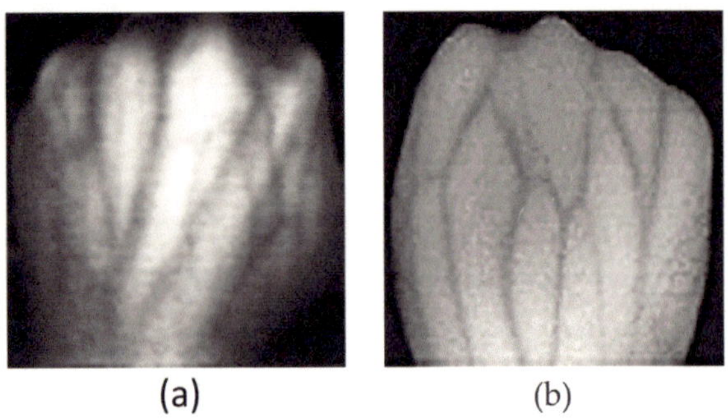

Figure 13. Dorsal vein images.

The second part of the feature vector is obtained by implementing an input image convolution operation with the bank of Gabor filters.

For each of the image, a filtration operation is carried out in accordance with Eq. (13) (**Figures 14–16**).

In the case of biometric identification of people based on texture features obtained using Gabor filter bank, we must solve the problem of a very large dimension of Gabor vector of traits.

	Figure 13a					Figure 13b				
	IDM	Contrast	Energy	Entropy	Corr.	IDM	Contrast	Energy	Entropy	Corr.
$d(1,0^{\circ})$	0.210	50.890	3.218E-4	8.368	2.271E-4	0.255	141.318	0.007	7.662	2.926E-4
$d(1,45^{\circ})$	0.173	67.564	2.622E-4	8.507	2.289E-4	0.218	198.051	0.006	7.794	2.932E-4
$d(1,90^{\circ})$	0.244	31.936	3.479E-4	8.218	2.268E-4	0.306	86.913	0.007	7.464	2.934E-4
$d(1,135^{\circ})$	0.146	80.621	2.375E-4	8.608	2.286E-4	0.214	199.180	0.006	7.803	2.931E-4
$d(2,0^{\circ})$	0,111	179.516	1.944E-4	8.804	2.265E-4	0.184	378.481	0.005	7.991	2.928E-4
$d(2,45^{\circ})$	0.102	206.593	1.757E-4	8.861	2.302E-4	0.161	456.028	0.004	8.065	3.010E-4
$d(2,90^{\circ})$	0.155	88.528	2.386E-4	8.581	2.273E-4	0.226	198.554	0.006	7.772	2.963E-4
$d(2,135^{\circ})$	0.078	288.156	1.626E-4	8.932	2.286E-4	0.161	459.783	0.004	8.075	3.002E-4

Table 3. Features calculated on the basis of co-occurrence matrix.

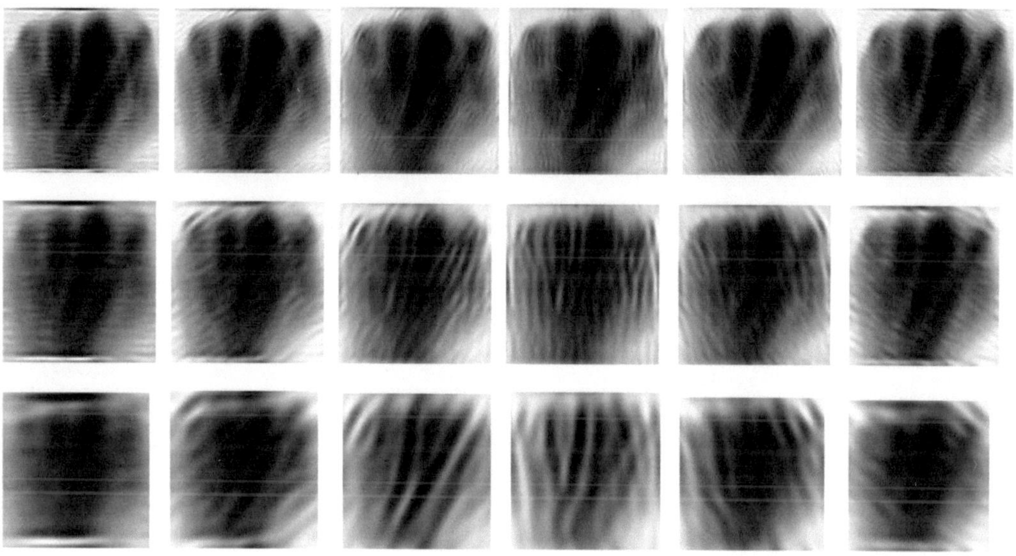

Figure 14. Real part of Gabor's filter responses of a hand dorsal image with **Figure 13**a. Rows correspond to scale (2, 4, 8), and columns to orientation $(0^{\circ}, 30^{\circ}, 60^{\circ}, 90^{\circ}, 120^{\circ}, 150^{\circ})$.

3.2. Reduction of dimension of the feature vector by the PCA method

In the case of the 128 × 128 image and 3 × 6 of Gabor's filter bank, the feature vector has a dimension of 128 × 128 × 3 × 6 = 294,912. The size of the feature is very correlated with each other; after down-sampling (according to factor 8), we get a vector of 36,864 elements or 2304 elements per image.

In order to reduce information redundancy, we use the principal component analysis (PCA) method. In some studies it is also called a Karhunen-Loeve discrete transform [29, 30].

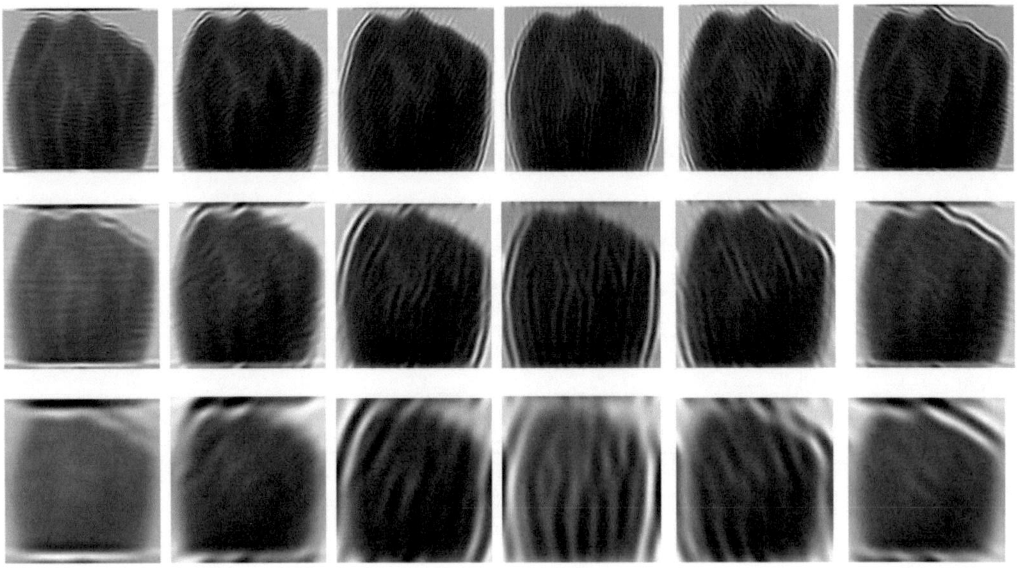

Figure 15. Real part of Gabor's filter responses of a hand dorsal image with **Figure 13**b. Rows correspond to scale (2, 4, 8), and columns to orientation $(0^{\circ}, 30^{\circ}, 60^{\circ}, 90^{\circ}, 120^{\circ}, 150^{\circ})$.

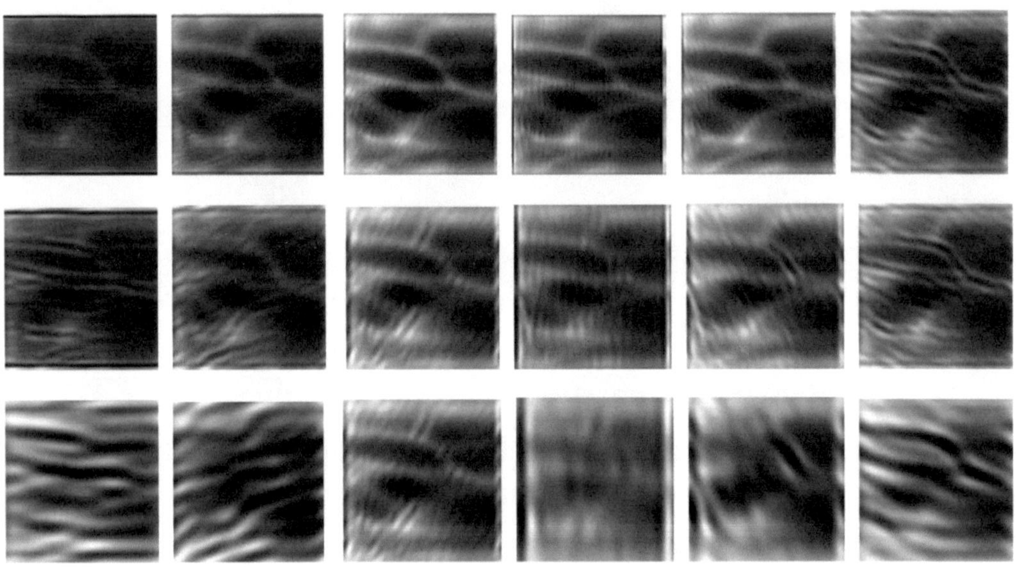

Figure 16. Real part of Gabor's filter responses of a wrist image with **Figure 12**f. Rows correspond to scale (2, 4, 8), and columns to orientation $(0^{\circ}, 30^{\circ}, 60^{\circ}, 90^{\circ}, 120^{\circ}, 150^{\circ})$.

The principal component analysis (PCA) method reduces the amount of data analyzed by subjecting them to linear transformation to a new coordinate system, resulting in new independent variables called the principal components.

The principal features of the PCA method are represented by eigenvectors. The eigenvectors of the covariance matrix are calculated based on the image training set and represent the principal components of the training image set.

We use two author's database of images of the blood vessel network, namely, a database of dorsal vein images and a database of wrist vein images containing 42 images created as part of a session with students and 58 images found in the resources of www. Each database had 100 images.

The collection of training images consisted of 50 images (50% of images from the student base and 50% of images from web sources).

The PCA algorithm is made as follows:

- Learning/training phase

The image $G_{\omega,\theta}(x,y)$ has $M \times N$ pixels and is converted into a $1 \times MN$ size vector. Images from the training set are presented in the form of a T matrix (**Figure 17**):

$$T = \left[G_1, G_2, \cdots, G_q\right] \tag{19}$$

where q is the number of images in the training set.

We calculate the mean image of all the images from the training database:

$$\Psi = \frac{1}{q}\sum_{1}^{q} G_q \tag{20}$$

Then, we calculate the difference between each image from the training database and the mean image:

$$\Phi_i = G_i - \Psi \tag{21}$$

The covariance matrix is defined as

$$C = \frac{1}{q}\sum_{1}^{q} \Phi_i\, \Phi_i^t = AA^t \tag{22}$$

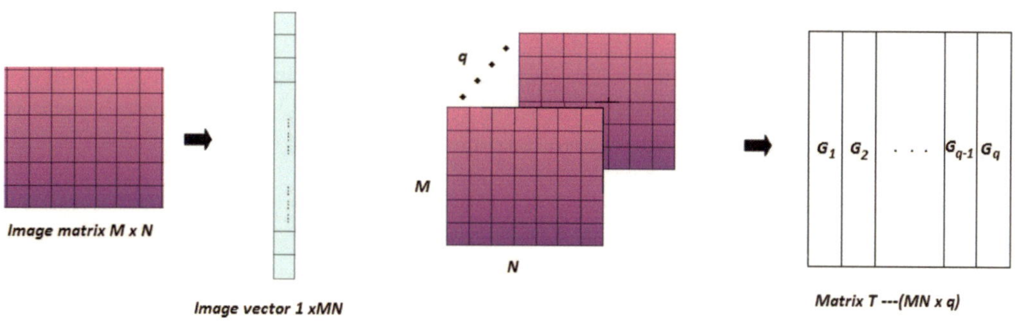

Figure 17. Image processing using PCA.

where

$$A = [\Phi_1, \ \Phi_2, \ \cdots, \ \Phi_q] \tag{23}$$

and matrix A has a dimension of $MN \times q$.

The covariance matrix has a dimension of $MN \times MN$.

Then, we calculate the eigenvalues and eigenvectors of the covariance matrix:

$$C\, v_i \ = \lambda_i v_i \qquad i = 1, \cdots, q \tag{24}$$

Then, we organize our eigenvectors according to their decreasing eigenvalues. We choose k principal components corresponding to k largest eigenvalues.

- Test/recognition phase

The new image is processed to obtain eigenvectors and eigenvalues. k the main components of the $\tilde{G}$ image are defined as

$$w = v^t \left(\tilde{G} - \Psi\right) \tag{25}$$

where $v = (v_1, \ v_2, \ \cdots, v_k)$.

Approximated image is calculated as

$$\overline{G} = vw + \Psi \tag{26}$$

We choose the k value according to the dependence:

$$\inf(k) = \frac{\sum_{1}^{k} \lambda_i}{\sum_{1}^{q} \lambda_i} \tag{27}$$

where k is the predefined number of eigenvectors and q the total number of eigenvectors.

A high value of k means that a large amount of input information will be stored, e.g., $\inf(k) \geq 0.99$ means that we retain 99% of information.

The variance of the first eigenvector is about 60% of the variance of the data set, the variance of the first 30 eigenvectors is about 85% of the variance of the data set, and 45 or more eigenvectors account for over 90% of the variance of the data set (**Figure 18**).

By increasing the number of eigenvectors, we increase the recognition efficiency.

We defined the vectors of features as follows:

$$FeatVect = (FV1, FV2) \tag{28}$$

where

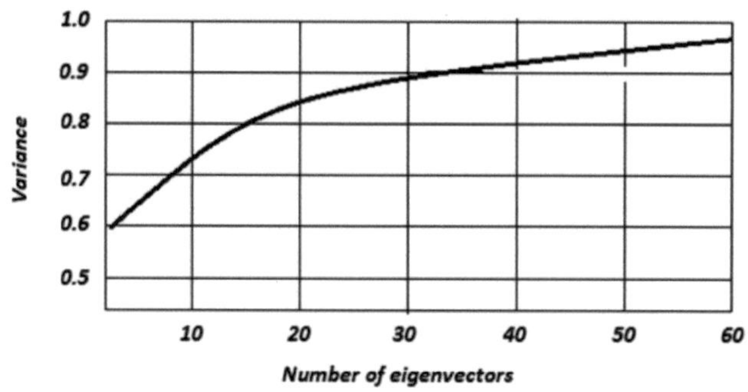

Figure 18. Variance as a function of the number of eigenvectors.

*FV*1 is Gabor's feature vector

*FV*2 is the co-occurrence feature vector

The quality of biometric systems is measured by two parameters: false acceptance rate *(FAR)* and false reject rate *(FRR). FAR* indicates the situation when the biometric input image is incorrectly accepted, and the *FRR* indicates the rejection of the user who should be correctly verified.

The size of the *FV1* vector has been set to 60 eigenvectors. The *featVect* size is 100. For these parameters *FRR* is 1.16% and *FAR* is 0.26%.

4. Conclusion

Recognition of people in biometric systems is based on the physiological or behavioral features that a person possesses.

In this chapter, we presented the image preprocessing operations used in static biometric systems (physiological modality). In particular, we discussed operations related to the transformation of the brightness scale of the image, modification of the brightness histogram, median filtering, edge detection, and image segmentation. In the course of these operations, we obtain an image enabling the extraction and measurement of features that serve as the basis for recognition.

Next, we discuss the feature extraction process, focusing on certain geometrical features and texture features. We present a representation of texture features based on parameters obtained from the co-occurrence matrix and images after Gabor's filtration with various scaling and orientation parameters. In terms of geometric features, we discuss the moment-based features and geometrical features based on the topological properties of the image.

We provide and discuss the feature extraction process in the images of the blood vessels of the hand dorsal and wrist. We present features calculated on the basis of matrix of co-occurrences and texture characteristics obtained using Gabor's filter bank. The process of reducing the dimensionality of a feature vector using the PCA method is also considered.

The main contributions of this chapter are the following:

- A set of information on image processing methods used in biometric systems
- Presentation of methods for obtaining feature vectors that are the basis of the process of recognizing people
- Explaining the problem of reducing the dimensionality of the feature vectors
- Showing parameters that are the basis for recognizing people based on images of the blood vessels of the hand dorsal and wrist

The chapter can be the basis for further studies and works on the image processing in biometric systems, especially based on images of the blood vessel network.

Author details

Ryszard S. Choras

Address all correspondence to: choras@utp.edu.pl

Institute of Telecommunications and Computer Sciences, UTP University of Science and Technology, Bydgoszcz, Poland

References

[1] Li SZ, Jain AK, editors. Encyclopedia of Biometrics. New York: Springer Science + Business Media; 2015

[2] Ross A, Nandakumar K, Jain AK. Handbook of Multibiometrics. New York: Springer; 2006

[3] Maltoni D, Maio D, Jain AK, Prabhakar S. Handbook of Fingerprint Recognition. New York: Springer; 2003

[4] Jain AK, Flynn PJ, Ross A, editors. Handbook of biometrics. New York: Springer; 2007

[5] Gonzales RC, Woods RE. Digital Image Processing. Upper Saddle River: Pearson Prentice Hall; 2008

[6] Zuiderveld K. Contrast Limited Adaptive Histogram Equalization. Cambridge: Academic; 1994

[7] Canny J. A computational approach to edge detection. IEEE Transactions on PAMI. 1986; **8**(6):769-789

[8] Haralick R, Shanmugam K, Dinstein I. Textural features for image classification. IEEE Transactions on Systems, Man, and Cybernetics. 1973;**SMC-3**(6):610-621

[9] Daugman JG. High confidence visual recognition of persons by a test of statistical independence. IEEE Transactions on Pattern Analysis and Machine Intelligence. 1993;**25**:1148-1161

[10] Haralick RM. Statistical and structural approaches to texture. IEEE Transactions on Systems, Man, and Cybernetics. 1979;**67**:786-804

[11] Gabor D. Theory of communication. Journal of Institution of Electrical Engineers. 1946;**93**:429-459

[12] Zhang H et al. Finger Vein Recognition Based on Gabor Filter. Intelligence Science and Big Data Engineering; 2013. pp. 827-834

[13] Choras RS. Iris-based person identification using Gabor wavelets and moments. In: Proceedings 2009 International Conference on Biometrics and Kansei Engineering ICBAKE; 2009. pp. 55-59

[14] Xueyan L, Shuxu G, Fengli G, Ye L. Vein pattern recognitions by moment invariants. In: Proceedings of the First International Conference on Bioinformatics and Biomedical Engineering; 2007. pp. 612-615

[15] Hu M. Pattern recognition by moment invariants. In: Proceedings of the IRE. 1969;**49**:1428

[16] Hong YH, Khotanzad A. Invariant image recognition by Zernike moments. IEEE Trans actions on PAMI. 1990;**12**(5):489-498

[17] Zhang T, Suen C. A fast parallel algorithm for thinning digital patterns. Communications of the ACM. 1984;**27**:236-239

[18] Kirbas C, Quek K. Vessel extraction techniques and algorithm: A survey. In: Proceedings of the 3rd IEEE Symposium on Bioinformatics and Bioengineering; 2003

[19] Kono M et al. Near-infrared finger vein patterns for personal identification. Applied Optics. 2002;**41**(35):7429-7436

[20] Ding Y, Zhuang D, Wang K. A study of hand vein recognition method. In: Proceedings of IEEE International Conference on Mechatronics & Automation; 2005. pp. 2106-2110

[21] Choras RS. Personal identification using forearm vein patterns. In: 2017 International Conference and Workshop on Bioinspired Intelligence (IWOBI); 2017. pp. 1-5

[22] Choras RS. Biometric personal authentication using images of forearm vein patterns. In: 2017 International Conference on Signals and Systems (ICSigSys); 2017. pp. 40-43

[23] Daugman JG. Complete discrete 2-D Gabor transforms by neural networks for image analysis and compression. IEEE Transactions on Acoustics, Speech, and Signal Processing. 1988;**36**:1169-1179

[24] Kang BJ et al. Multimodal biometric method based on vein and geometry of a single finger. IET Computer Vision. 2010;**4**(3):209-217

[25] Kumar A, Prathyusha KV. Personal authentication using hand vein triangulation and knuckle shape. IEEE Transactions on Image Processing. 2009;**18**:2127-2136

[26] Lee EC et al. New finger biometric method using near infrared imaging. Sensors. 2011;**11**: 2319-2333

[27] Wang Y, Li K, Cui J. Hand-dorsa vein recognition based on partition local binary pattern. In: IEEE 10th International Conference on Signal Processing (ICSP); 2010. pp. 1671-1674

[28] Tanaka T, Kubo N. Biometric authentication by hand vein patterns. In: Proceedings of SICE Annual Conference; 2004. pp. 249-253

[29] Liu CJ, Wechsler H. Gabor feature based classification using the enhanced fisher linear discriminant model for face recognition. IEEE Transactions on Image Processing. 2002; **11**(4):467-476

[30] Tao J, Jiang W, Gao Z, Chen S, Wang C. Palmprint recognition based on 2-dimension PCA. In: First International Conference on Innovative Computing, Information and Control; 2006;**1**:326-330

Chapter 7

A Human Body Mathematical Model Biometric Using Golden Ratio: A New Algorithm

Evon Abu-Taieh and Hamed S. Al-Bdour

Additional information is available at the end of the chapter

http://dx.doi.org/10.5772/intechopen.76113

Abstract

This research provides more than 35 measurements rules derived from the perspectives of Vitruvian Man and Neufert and their basis of the golden proportion, to build a human body model on computers for the use of multimedia. The measurements are based on 25 proportional rules derived from 15 proportions given by Vitruvian Man and 29 golden proportions in Bauentwurfslehre by Ernst Neufert. Furthermore, the research will suggest two algorithms to calculate the 67 measurements with precision; assuming that the algorithms output will be used as guideline to human body modelers in simulation, gaming, plastic surgery, as well as the world of biometrics or wherever human body measurements and calculations is needed like prosthetic limbs, spatial design, and machine learning of human biometrics. Furthermore, building proportional models creates visual harmony in measurements and visual parity model. Hence, the chapter facilitates and explains for the human modeler the process of human modeling from within an algorithm. This research is an expanded work based on two published conference papers listed in the references section.

Keywords: simulation, multimedia, computer, medial section, divine proportion, golden proportion, mean of Phidias, Neufert, human biometrics, divine proportion, multimedia, human modeling, machine learning

1. Introduction

This research is based on two published papers [16, 17] pertaining to same subject by the same author. The research identifies more than 35 measurements and proportions to be used in modeling a human body on computers. The 35 measurements rules are based on Vitruvian Man and Neufert descriptions of *Bauentwurfslehre* by Ernst Neufert [20] and Leonardo da

Vincicirca both based on the golden proportion notion. First, the research gives an introduction about golden proportion known also as golden section. Then, in the second section, the research explains the three dimensions of golden proportion: mathematically, geometrically, and arithmetically. The third section of the research presents the work of FIBONACCI and his series in the golden proportion. Followed by a discussion of the geometry of Golden ratio and the essential proportions in Vitruvian Man, in the fourth section, where 15 essential proportions are explained based on the Vitruvian Man. In fifth section, BAUENTWURFSLEHRE by ERNST NEUFERT [20] is further explained with circle geometry and 29 golden proportions are reflected in the work. In the sixth section, the face and hand proportions in relation to the golden proportion are further explained. Based on the findings of the previous sections, the seventh section suggests two algorithms to be used when building a human body model. Thereby, presenting more than 35 proportions and measurements used to model human body model along with a simple algorithm that calculates exact measurements. As such, the research facilitates and explains for the human modeler the process of human modeling in multimedia arena. Hence, this research will be a spring board for researchers, practitioners in human modeling in multimedia field.

Dubbed by the Greeks, "Golden Ratio" is a mathematical relation and proportion, where the length to width of a rectangle proportion is 1:1.61803398874989484820, such proportion is most suited for human eye and is used by architects, artists, sculptures in their work. While the Golden Ration does not embody every structure or pattern in the universe, yet, historically, this ratio emerged in Great Pyramid of Giza/Khufu/Cheops (2560 BC) [21], and in Vitruvian Man by Leonardo da Vinci and Neufert. More notably, in today's multimedia, Golden Ratio is used in many applications: plastic surgery simulation software, animation software, art, architecture, sculpture, anatomy. A close exploration of such divine proportion and the related applications, offers opportunities to connect an understanding the conceptions of ratio and proportion to the geometry, proportions, and ratio related to the Vitruvian Man and its relation to Bauentwurfslehre by Ernst Neufert (1936) [20]. Throughout the next sections, a detailed explanation will be given to golden ratio: geometrically, mathematically, and arithmetically.

2. Golden ratio

Golden Ratio has many perspectives: geometrically, mathematically, and arithmetically. A full understanding of all perspectives as well as the origin of the term is essential, in order to grasp the magnitude from the microscale to the macroscale. In this section, *Golden Ratio* will be explained term and perspective wise.

The origin of the term *Golden Ratio* was termed by Phidias. Phidias is a Greek painter, sculptor, and architect. Phidias sculpted the famous Zeus at temple of Olympia, which was considered one of the Seven Wonders of the World. The *golden ratio* was termed *mean of Phidias* [6, 8, 15]. There are many terms that reflect the term Golden Ratio: *golden mean* [2, 7, 10] and *extreme/mean ratio,* (Euclid) *medial section* [3], *divine proportion, divine section* (Latin: sectio divina), *golden proportion, golden cut,* [11] *golden number* [6, 15, 8]. In current history, G*olden Ratio* was termed as

http://dx.doi.org/10.5772/intechopen.76113

Golden Section (goldene Schnitt) by a German mathematician named Martin Ohm who lived from 1792 till 1872. Mark Barr coined the term (phi) to reflect the idea of *Golden ratio,* in commemoration of Phidias, because many historians [7, 13] claim that Phidias used the Golden Ratio in his sculptures.

Simply, *Golden Ratio* is a proportion of two unequal segments: the proportion of the long segment to the short segment is equal to the total of the two segments to the long segment, both equal 1:1.61803398874989. In **Figure 1**, the longer segment *a* and the short segment *b*, whereby the proportion of *a*:*b* is equal to the total of *a* and *b* to *a*. The number 1.61803398874989 is the value of *phi*. In this context, the ensuing question is how to derive *b* from *a* while keeping the Golden Proportion, *phi*?

To derive the *b* segment from the *a* segment, the following must be conducted: First, draw a square with length *a,* as articulated in **Figure 2**, and construct a unit square. Then, at midpoint on the side of the square, draw a line to the opposite side. Next, connect the midpoint to an opposite corner. When using that line as the radius to draw an arc, accordingly, the long dimension of the rectangle is defined.

The simpler picture is reflected in **Figure 3** where the "*a*" and the "*b*" are shown and the both hold the value of *phi,* the Golden proportion.

Concluding the section where the origin of the term *Golden Ratio* was not only clarified but thorough explanation of the geometrical aspect of the ratio was also put forward, in order to comprehend the magnitude of this proportion.

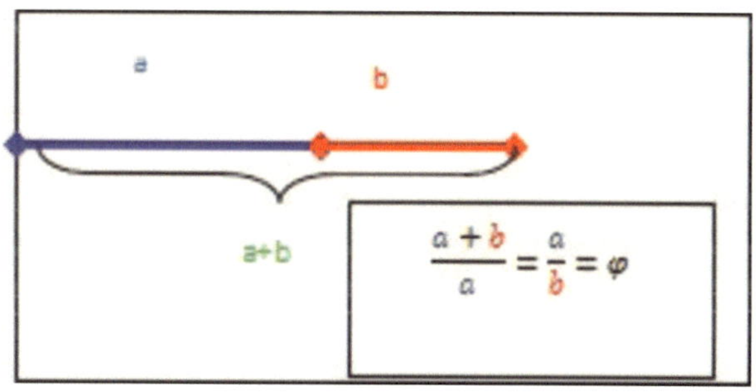

Figure 1. The *Golden Ratio* represented in line segments [3, 4].

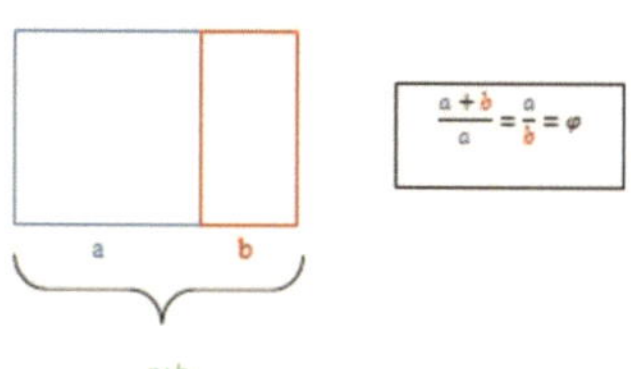

Figure 2. Construction of a golden rectangle.

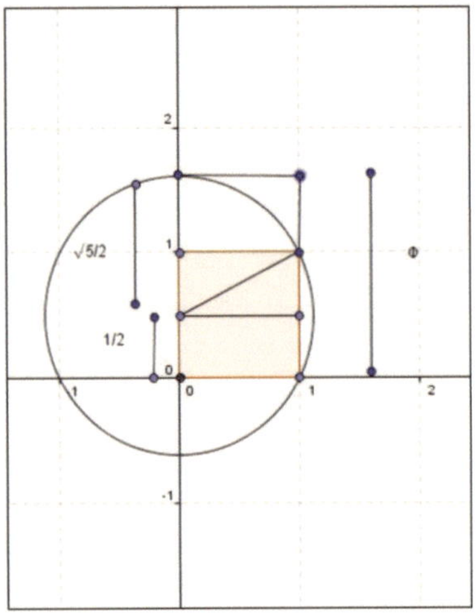

Figure 3. A golden rectangle with longer side *a* and shorter segment *b*.

3. The mathematics of golden ratio: Fibonacci series

In view that understanding the golden ratio mathematics is imminent, especially when it is reflected in the Fibonacci Series [2]. Another perspective is the how the *golden ration* interrelates with the square root of 5. The two perspectives are clarified in the next paragraphs. Accordingly, this section will discuss the mathematical properties of golden ratio (*Phi*), especially in Fibonacci series, while noting that *phi* with small letter p is equal to 1.618033988749895, whereas *Phi* with capital P equals 0.618033988749895.

Fibonacci series, named after Leonardo Fibonacci, is a simple series that when starting with 0 and 1, each new number in the series is simply the sum of the two before it. The ratio of each successive pair of numbers in the series approximates *phi* (1.618). In fact, after the 40th number in the series, the ratio is accurate to 15 decimal places. Furthermore, the value of golden ratio (*phi*) is reciprocal to the value of golden ratio (*Phi*), noting that the ratios of the successive numbers in the Fibonacci series quickly converge on golden ratio (*Phi*), the ratio is accurate to 15 decimal places:

$$\mathrm{f_n} = Phi^{\mathrm{n}}/5^{½}$$

For example, the 40th number in the Fibonacci series is 102,334,155, which can be computed as (**Table 1**):

$$\mathrm{f_{40}} = Phi^{40}/5^{½} = 102,334,155$$

Concluding this section, where the mathematical perspective of the Golden Ratio was illustrated through the Fibonacci Series and the relationship of the successive elements of the series that converge to the golden ratio.

n	F_n	F_{n+1}	phi	Phi
0	0	1	infinity	0
1	1	2	2	0.5
2	3	5	1.666666667	0.6
3	8	13	1.62500000000000	0.615384615384615
4	21	34	1.61904761904762	0.617647058823529
5	55	89	1.61818181818182	0.617977528089888
6	144	233	1.61805555555556	0.618025751072961
7	377	610	1.61803713527851	0.618032786885246
8	987	1597	1.61803444782168	0.618033813400125
9	2584	4181	1.61803405572755	0.618033963166707
10	6765	10,946	1.61803399852180	0.618033985017358
11	17,711	28,657	1.61803399017560	0.618033988205325
12	46,368	75,025	1.61803398895790	0.618033988670443
13	121,393	196,418	1.61803398878024	0.618033988738303
14	317,811	514,229	1.61803398875432	0.618033988748204
15	832,040	1,346,269	1.61803398875054	0.618033988749648
16	2,178,309	3,524,578	1.61803398874999	0.618033988749859
17	5,702,887	9,227,465	1.61803398874991	0.618033988749890
18	14,930,352	24,157,817	1.61803398874990	0.618033988749894
19	39,088,169	63,245,986	1.61803398874990	0.618033988749895
20	102,334,155	165,580,141	1.61803398874989	0.618033988749895
21	267,914,296	433,494,437	1.61803398874989	0.618033988749895
22	701,408,733	1,134,903,170	1.61803398874989	0.618033988749895
23	1,836,311,903	2,971,215,073	1.61803398874989	0.618033988749895
24	4,807,526,976	7,778,742,049	1.61803398874989	0.618033988749895
25	12,586,269,025	20,365,011,074	1.61803398874989	0.618033988749895
26	32,951,280,099	53,316,291,173	1.61803398874989	0.618033988749895

Table 1. Fibonacci series converge on Phi.

4. Vitruvian man

Proportions used to model, paint, and sculpt a human body are essential, as [18] Luca Pacioli, a contemporary of Da Vinci, indicates that "without mathematics there is no art," proportions are an integral part of design and beauty of nature, to achieve beauty, balance, and harmony, thereby presenting visual parity to the audience. According to [9], such use of proportion creates *the greatest harmony in the symmetrical relations.*

The use of proportions when drawing a human body is not new, in fact, Leonardo da Vinci suggested a 15 rules of proportions which will be discussed in this section. Also, Marcus Vitruvius Pollio (born c. 80–70 BC, died after c. 15 BC), named by Taylor in an article in The New Zealand Herald called Marcus Vitruvius Pollio "the world's first known engineer" [12]. Marcus Vitruvius Pollio wrote his work *On Architecture* in 25 BC. In his book, he stated that *human body and a perfect building are similar* [1]. Furthermore, the use of proportion in buildings, paintings, and sculpting is not a new idea so is the use of human body proportions in buildings.

Leonardo da Vinci developed 15 proportion rules used to model a human in his work named VITRUVIAN MAN. The famous proportions were written underneath the illustration shown in **Figure 4**. The rules are further explained in **Figure 5** and in the list of proportions shown at the end of this section.

The first rule is that the length of a man is equal to the width of a man with both arms extended. Hence, a man can be inscribed in a square, as seen in **Figure 4**. A man can be inscribed in circle where the extended arms while raised to the level of the head and both feet are on the circumstance of the circle, as seen in **Figure 4**.

The second rule is for the proportion of the face which is 1/10 of the man height. The third rule is for the head proportion which is 1/8 of man height. The fourth and fifth rules, from the chest to the hair line is 1/7-man height, and from chest to the head is 1/6-man height. The sixth rule pertains to the shoulders width, which is ¼ of man height. The seventh rule measures the distance from breast to the top of the head and the proportion is ¼ of the man height, noting

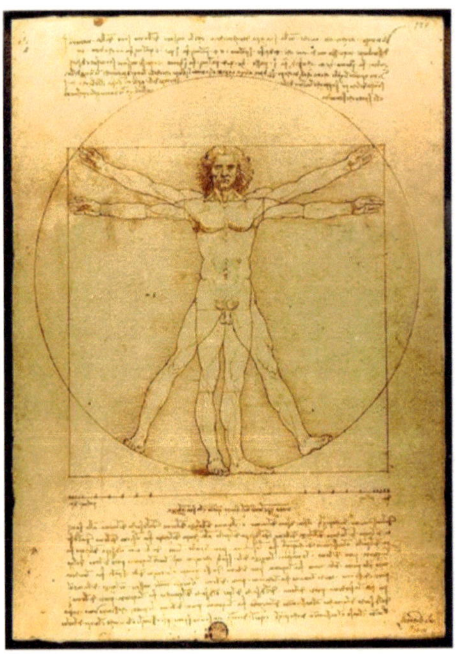

Figure 4. Vitruvian man by Leonardo da Vinci, Galleria dell' Accademia, Venice (1485–1490).

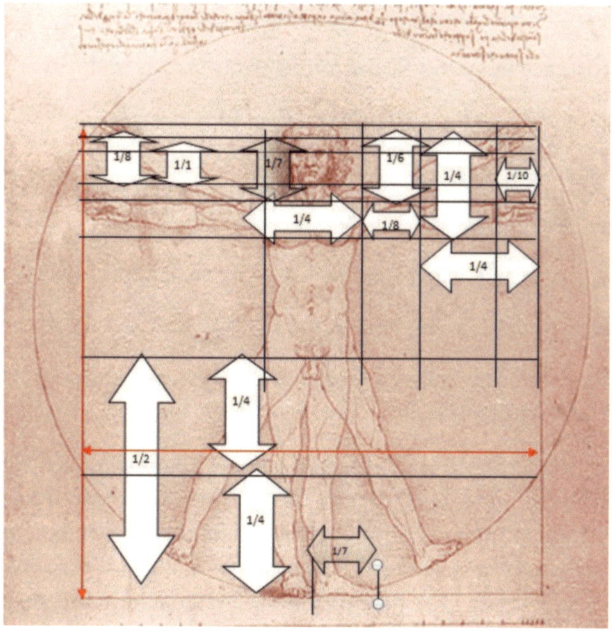

Figure 5. Vitruvian man with proportions suggested by Leonardo da Vinci.

that measurements from the rule 6 and 7 correlate. Rules 8–10 all relate to forearm, upper arm, and hand which are ¼, 1/8, and 1/10 height of a man, respectively. It is worthwhile to note that the aforementioned three rules on measurement of forearm, shoulders width correlate with rule 7. Rule 11 is the measure of half the man, from the root of the penis to the top of the head or the root of the penis to the sole of the feet is ½ of man height. Rules 12–14 pertain to foot leg and thigh. The foot is 1/6 of man height while the leg and thigh are both equal to ¼ of man height. The last rule explains proportions used in the face which divides the face to three-thirds: one-third from hair line to eyebrows, second third from eyebrows to below nose, and from below the nose to end of chin. The last rule, pertaining to face proportions will be thoroughly discussed in Section 6 of this chapter. The original quote from Leonardo da Vinci work is in the research [16, 17].

In short, [5], the following table summarized the previous quote as illustrated in **Figure 5**.

1. The length of the outspread arms is equal to the height of a man.
2. *Face*: from the hairline to the bottom of the chin is 1/10 of the height of a man.
3. *Head*: from below the chin to the top of the head is 1/8 of the height of a man.
4. From above the chest to the top of the head is 1/6 of the height of a man.
5. From above the chest to the hairline is 1/7 of the height of a man.
6. *Shoulders*: the maximum width of the shoulders is ¼ of the height of a man.
7. From the breasts to the top of the head is ¼ of the height of a man.

8. *Forearm*: The distance from the elbow to the tip of the hand is ¼ of the height of a man.

9. *Upper arm*: the distance from the elbow to the armpit is 1/8 of the height of a man.

10. *Hand*: the length of the hand is 1/10 of the height of a man.

11. The root of the penis is at 1/2 the height of a man.

12. *Foot*: is 1/6 of the height of a man.

13. *Leg*: from below the foot to below the knee is ¼ of the height of a man.

14. *Thigh*: from below the knee to the root of the penis is ¼ of the height of a man.

15. Face: the distances from the below the chin to the nose and the eyebrows and the hairline are equal to the ears and to 1/3 of the face.

In closing, this section attempted to shed light on the significance of using the divine proportions in design, beauty, and parity. Famous and profound painters, designers over the centuries have been influenced to use proportion when painting and sculpting human body; in this context, 15 proportional rules used by Leonardo da Vinci in drawing the Vitruvian Man was explicitly discussed, noting that proportion use was extended to be used in architecture and by architects like Marcus Vitruvius Pollio, which will be further discussed next. As such, proportion use in art is equally profound and archaic.

5. Bauentwurfslehre by Ernst Neufert

Bauentwurfslehre is a German word means *Architects' Data* a book authored by Ernst Neufert a German engineer. *Architects' Data* is reference book for spatial requirements. The author developed the book based on the previous work of Leonardo da Vinci with *golden ratio* proportions. In this section, the work of *Bauentwurfslehre* by Ernst Neufert is first explained. Then 29 proportional rules are derived to further the work of the algorithm that is being developed to provide 35 measures that helps building a human model.

The *Bauentwurfslehre* shown in **Figure 6** is the composed of 29 proportional measurements, named m (in small letter) and M (capital letter) used on a human model. Also, there are 12 circles to derive the proportions. Both the circles and the proportions will be explained in the next paragraphs.

The 12 circles are numbered to explain each and differentiate one from the other. To build the model in **Figure 6**, the following steps are done: (1) a square is sketched with height of the man as the height of the square as well as the width; (2) two lines are sketched from opposite corners to locate the center of the first circle (the biggest circle); (3) a second circle is drawn with center is the navel and the radius is extended from navel to perpendicular line drawn from hand rest to ground; (4) a third circle is sketched with the navel as the center, and the radius is distance from navel to perpendicular line extended from elbow to ground; (5) a fourth

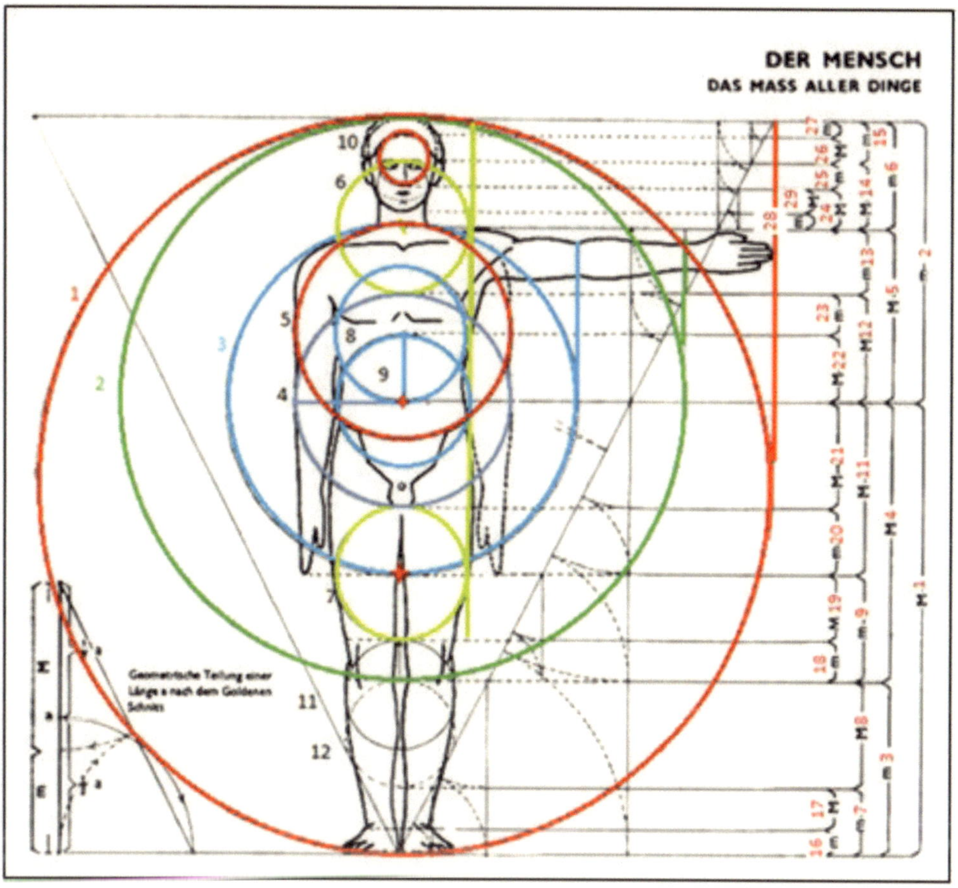

Figure 6. Bauentwurfslehre by Ernst Neufert (1936) [14].

circle is drawn with the navel as center and the radius from navel to the outer side of the arm; (6) a fifth circle is drawn with the center is mid-chest center, with radius outer arms; (7) a sixth circle is centered in the throat and the radius from throat to the line extended from shoulder to the ground; (8) a seventh circle is sketched with center in mid thighs and the radius is the outer side of the thigh; (9) an eighth circle is sketched and centered in the is mid-chest center, with radius inside arms.; (10) a ninth circle is sketched and centered in the navel and the radius is the sides of the middle section; (11) a tenth circle is drawn and centered in the point between the eyes and the radius is the sides of the face (temples); (12) the eleventh circle is drawn and centered to touch the seventh circle while reducing the radius to the outer side of the legs, below the knee, and finally (13) the twelfth circle is sketched similar to circle 11 while touching the second circle.

To explain the golden ratio from within the 29 measurements little m and big M, one must start with explaining the base case M16. The measurement *M16* is measured from bottom of foot to foot end (see **Figure 7**). *M17* is derived according to the golden ratio rule seen in (1):

$$\frac{M17 + M16}{M17} = \frac{M17}{M16} = \varphi \tag{1}$$

Furthermore, *M7* is the total of both *M16* and *M17* [see (2)]. In addition, *M7* is used to derive *M8* according to golden ratio rule as illustrated in Eq. (3). Note that the upper limit of *M8* is below the knee and it is the tangent of both *circles 12* and *2* (see **Figure 6**). Also, note that *M3* is the total of *M7* and *M8* as seen in Eq. (4):

$$\mathrm{M7} = \mathrm{M16} + \mathrm{M17} \tag{2}$$

$$\frac{M8 + M7}{M8} = \frac{M8}{M7} = \varphi \tag{3}$$

$$\mathrm{M3} = \mathrm{M7} + \mathrm{M8} \tag{4}$$

Again, *M18* is the measure of the knee, below knee to above the knee. The *M18* is used to derive *M19* according to rule in Eq. (5). The upper limit of *M19* is the center of *circle 7* and tangent to *circle 3* also, if a line drawn with the hand extended on the sides. In addition, note that *M9* is the total of *M18* and *M19* see (6):

$$\frac{M19 + M18}{M19} = \frac{M19}{M18} = \varphi \tag{5}$$

$$\mathrm{M9} = \mathrm{M18} + \mathrm{M19} \tag{6}$$

The *M9* is used to derive *M11* = M9 × 1.61803398874989. The *M20* is the measure of length of the hand (tip of figure to rest). The *M20* is used to derive *M21* according to golden ratio rule in (7). The upper limit of *M20* and the lower limit of *M21* is tangent to *circles 7* and *4* (see **Figure 6**). The upper limit of *M21* is tangent to *circle 8* and the center of *circle 9* and crosses the navel:

$$\frac{M21 + M20}{M21} = \frac{M21}{M20} = \varphi \tag{7}$$

The upper limit of *M11* is tangent to *circle 8* and the center of *circle 9* and crosses the navel. And *M11* is the addition of *M20* and *M21* (see **Figure 6**). *M11* is driven from *M9* according to rule in **Figure 3**:

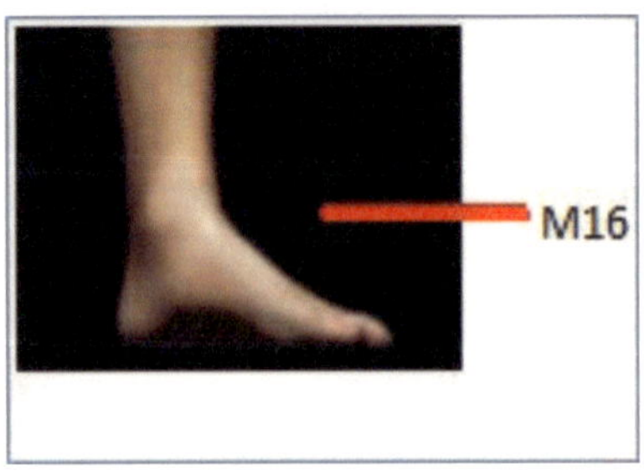

Figure 7. Limit of M16.

http://dx.doi.org/10.5772/intechopen.76113

$$\mathrm{M11} = \mathrm{M20} + \mathrm{M21}. \tag{8}$$

The upper limit of *M4* is tangent to *circle 8* and the center of *circle 9* and crosses the navel. *M4* is the addition of *M9* and *M11* (see **Figure 6**). Also, M4 is driven according to rules explained in **Figure 3** and as seen in (9):

$$\mathrm{M4} = \mathrm{M9} + \mathrm{M11} \tag{9}$$

$$\frac{M4 + M3}{M4} = \frac{M4}{M3} = \varphi \tag{10}$$

$$\mathrm{M1} = \mathrm{M3} + \mathrm{M4} \tag{11}$$

Once you reach the navel, one can easily calculate M2 According to (12). The M27 is from top of the head to hair line tip. The M27 is used to derive M26 according to rules explained in **Figure 3**. The lower limit of M27 is tangent to circle 10, while the lower limit of M26 is tangent to circle 6 and crosses the center of circle 10 (see **Figure 6**). Again, to derive M26 apply:

$$\frac{M1 + M2}{M1} = \frac{M1}{M2} = \varphi \tag{12}$$

According to (13), the M2 is the addition of M6 and M5. Hence, both M6 and M5 can be driven from M2 according to (14) and (15). The upper limit of M2 is tangent for circles 1 and 2. The M2 lower limit crosses center of circle 9 which is the navel (see **Figure 6**).

$$\mathrm{M2} = \mathrm{M6} + \mathrm{M5} \tag{13}$$

$$M5 = \frac{M2}{\varphi} \tag{14}$$

$$M6 = \frac{M2}{\varphi + 1} \tag{15}$$

The M6 is from the base of the throat to the top of the head. Since M6 is the total of M14 and M15 according to (16). Hence, M14, and M15 can be driven according to (17) and (18):

$$\mathrm{M6} = \mathrm{M15} + \mathrm{M14} \tag{16}$$

$$M14 = \frac{M6}{\varphi} \tag{17}$$

$$m15 = \frac{M6}{\varphi + 1} \tag{18}$$

The M5 is from the navel to the throat, the upper limit of M5 is same level as center of circle 6. Since M5 is the total of M13 and M12 according to (16). Hence, M12, and M13 can be driven according to (20) and (21):

$$\mathrm{M5} = \mathrm{M13} + \mathrm{M12} \tag{19}$$

$$M12 = \frac{M5}{\varphi} \tag{20}$$

$$M13 = \frac{M5}{\varphi + 1} \tag{21}$$

The M12 is from the navel to rib cage, the upper limit of M12 is same level as tangent to of circle 4. Since M12 is the total of M23 and M22 according to (22). Hence, M22, and M23 can be driven according to (23) and (24):

$$\mathrm{M12} = \mathrm{M23} + \mathrm{M22} \tag{22}$$

$$M22 = \frac{M12}{\varphi} \tag{23}$$

$$M23 = \frac{M12}{\varphi + 1} \tag{24}$$

The M15 is from eyebrows to top of the head, the upper limit of M12 is same level as tangent to of circle 6. Since M12 is the total of M27 and M26 according to (25). Hence, M26, and M27 can be driven according to (26) and (27):

$$\mathrm{M15} = \mathrm{M27} + \mathrm{M26} \tag{25}$$

$$M26 = \frac{M15}{\varphi} \tag{26}$$

$$M27 = \frac{M15}{\varphi + 1} \tag{27}$$

The M14 is from the throat to eyebrows. M14 is tangent to circles 3 and 5 while the upper limit is tangent to circle 6. Note that, *M14* is the addition of *M24* and *M25*, and is derived according (29) and (30):

$$\mathrm{M14} = \mathrm{M24} + \mathrm{M25} \tag{28}$$

$$M24 = \frac{M14}{\varphi} \tag{29}$$

$$M25 = \frac{M14}{\varphi + 1} \tag{30}$$

The *M24* upper limit will be tangent to *circle 10* and the lower limit is tangent to *circle 5*. M24 is tangent to circles 3 and 5 while the upper limit is tangent to circle 6. Note that, M24 is the addition of *M29* and *M28*, and is derived according (32) and (33):

http://dx.doi.org/10.5772/intechopen.76113

$$M24 = M29 + M28 \tag{31}$$

$$M29 = \frac{M24}{\varphi} \tag{32}$$

$$M28 = \frac{M24}{\varphi + 1} \tag{33}$$

This section explained 29 proportions and 12 circles used in Bauentwurfslehre by Ernst Neufert. The section first explained the work which is based on Leonardo da Vinci with golden ratio proportions. Then the research explained each circle's radius and center. Next, the research explained each proportion and how to calculate each ratio from M1 to M29. The findings of this section will be reflected in the algorithm suggested in Section 7 of this research. The next section will discuss the golden proportions used to model a human face and hands.

6. Face and hand proportions

The golden proportion is repeated in the human face and is used by plastic surgeons to follow as guidelines. Human face from the bottom of the chin to the hairline in length to the edge of the eyebrow is 1:1.618 or 1: φ as illustrated in **Figure 12**, the red rectangle. Likewise, proportion is illustrated in the same figure using the green rectangle; the green rectangle is edges of the eyebrows and the height is from the tip of the nose to the top of the eyebrows. The third golden proportion is seen in the blue rectangle. The blue rectangle extends from the eyebrow to the bottom lip, and from the space between the eyes to the end of the eyebrow. Based on the previous one can calculate the width of the face to equal 1: length of the face. The length of the face = M26 + M25 + M29 and the length of the green box equals M25 and the length of the blue rectangle is 2 × M25. Once the length is calculated, then the width can be easily calculated (**Figure 8**).

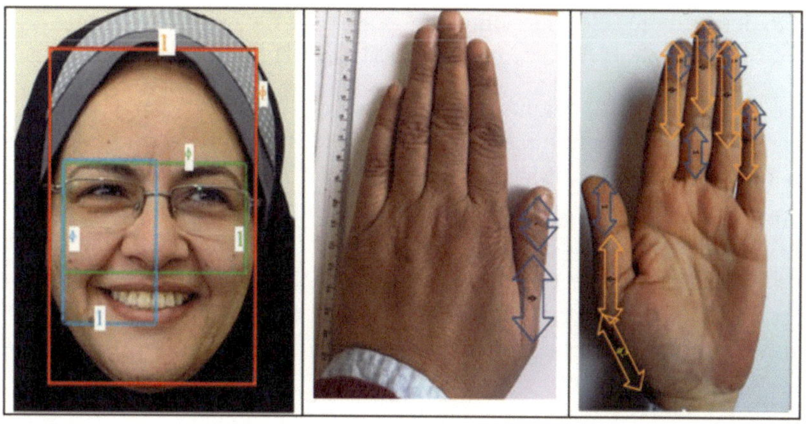

Figure 8. Face and hand golden proportions.

Gary Meisner [19] lists seven vertical golden proportions in the face and eight horizontal golden proportions. Next, the 15 proportions will be described based on Meisner's guide to beauty. The seven vertical golden proportions are: center of pupils to bottom of chin the golden ratio point is at center of lips, center of pupils to bottom of chin the golden ratio point is at nose at nostrils, center of pupils to nose base the golden ratio point is at nose flair top, top arc of eyebrows to bottom of eyes the golden ratio point is at top of eyes, center of pupils to center of lips the golden ratio point is at nose at nostrils, top of lips to bottom of lips the golden ratio point is at center of lips, nose at nostrils to center of lips the golden ratio point is at top of lips. Eight horizontal golden proportions are: side of face to opposite side of face, the golden ratio point is at inside of near eye; side of face to inside of opposite eye, the golden ratio point is at inside of near eye; center of face to side of face, the golden ratio point is at outside edge of eye; side of face to inside edge of eye, the golden ratio point is at outside edge of eye; side of face to outside edge of eye, the golden ratio point is at outside of eyebrow; center of face to width of mouth, the golden ratio point is at width of nose; side of mouth to opposite side of mouth, the golden ratio point is at cupid's bow. Meisner designated 33 points on human face as seen in [19], such points can be driven from the derived rules in **Figure 9**, namely *the length of the face = M25 + M26 + M29 and the width of the face = length of face/1.618.* Since the width and length of face are known then Meisner's points (1, 33, 19, 20) can be calculated: Meisner's points (1, 33) are the upper and lower limit of the face height, respectively. Meisner's points (19, 20) are the left and right limits of the width of the face respectively. Meisner's point (15) = width of face/2.618 and Meisner's point (16) = width of face/2.618 both according to H1 and H2 in Meisner's work [19]. Meisner's points (13, 14) can be calculated as follows: Meisner's point (13) = width of face/(2 × 2.618) same for Meisner's point (14) = width of face/ (2 × 2.618). Meisner's point (7) = Meisner's point (13)/1.618 and Meisner's point (8) = Meisner's point (14)/ 1.618). Meisner's point (29) = width of face / (2 × 1.618) and Meisner's point (30) = width of face/ (2 × 1.618). Meisner's Point (24) = half width of face to Meisner's point (30)/1.618 and Meisner's point (23) = half width of face to Meisner's point (30)/1.618. Meisner's points (27,28) are cupid bow hence to derive them divide the distance from Meisner's point (29–30) over golden ration, Meisner's point (29, 30) = distance Meisner's point (29, 30) × 1.618. According to the previous 12 golden ratio rules were derived to the face vertically. Next, the same will be conducted to derive more rules horizontally. Again, since the height of the face is known, one can derive seven golden ratio rules according to Meisner [19].

First Meisner's points (19, 20) heights: Meisner's point (19) height = length of face/ (1 + 1.618) and Meisner's point (20) height = face length/ (1 + 1.618). Meisner's points (21, 22) are calculated from bottom as follows: Meisner's point (21) = face length/1.618 and the same for Meisner's point (22) = face length/1.618. Meisner's points (3, 4) measuring from bottom are face length/1.618, hence Meisner's point (3) = face length/1.618 and m Meisner's point (4) = face length/1.618. Meisner's points (11, 12) the center of the pupils are calculated as follows: Meisner's point (12) = difference of height between Meisner's point (20) and Meisner's point (4)/1.618 from top, and Meisner's point (11) = difference of height between Meisner's point (19) and Meisner's point (3) /1.618 from top. Meisner's point (31) is calculated as follows Meisner's point (31) = from Meisner's point (11, 12) to Meisner's point (33)/ (1 + 1.618). Meisner's points (23, 24) are calculated as follows: Meisner's point (23) = from Meisner's point (11, 12) to

Input M16
*Set M17 = M16 * 1.618*
Set M7 = M16 + M17
*Set M8 = M7 * 1.618*
Set M3 = M7 + M8
*Set M4 = M3 * 1.618*
Set M9 = M4/2.618
*Set M11 = M4-M9 or M11 = M9 * 1.618*
Set M18 = M9/2.618
Set M19 = M9/1.618 or M19 = M18-M9
Set M20 = M11/2.618
Set M21 = M11/1.618 orM21 = M11-M21
Set M1 = M3 + M4
{above the navel}
Set M2 = M1/1.618
Set M5 = M2/1.618
Set M6 = M2/2.618
Set M13 = M5/2.618
Set M12 = M5/1.618
Set M22 = M12/1.618
Set M23 = M12/2.618
Set M14 = M6/2.618
Set M15 = M6/1.618
Set M24 = M14/2.618
Set M25 = M14/1.618
Set M29 = M24/1.618
Set M28 = M24/2.618
Set M26 = M15/1.618
Set M27 = M15/2.618
Set Total height = M1 + M2
The length of the face = M25 + M26 + M29
The width of the face = length of face/1.618
*Left tip of eye brow to the right tip of eye brow = M25 * 1.618*
*From tip of eye brow to between the eyes = 2 * M25 / 1.618*
Width of shoulders 1/4 of height of a man
The foot is 1/6 of the height of a man

Figure 9. Human body measurements algorithm.

Meisner's point (33)/ (1 + 1.618) and Meisner's point (24) = from Meisner's point (11, 12) to Meisner's point (33)/ (1 + 1.618). Meisner's point (2) is calculated as follows: Meisner's point (2) = from Meisner's point (11, 12) to Meisner's point (33)/ (1 + 1.618), measuring from the top. To calculate Meisner's points (9, 10), the following must be done: Meisner's point (9) = difference from Meisner's point (3) to Meisner's point (19)/1.618 and Meisner's point (10) = difference from Meisner's point (4) to Meisner's point (20)/1.618. Meisner's point (17) = difference from Meisner's point (9) to Meisner's point (19)/1.618 and Meisner's point (18) = difference from Meisner's point (10) to Meisner's point (20)/1.618. Meisner's point (5) = difference from Meisner's point (3) to Meisner's point (7)/1.618 and Meisner's point (6) = difference from

Meisner's point (4) to Meisner's point (8)/1.618 from the top. Meisner's point (32) = the difference between Meisner's point (33) to Meisner's point (31)/1.618 from bottom. The Meisner's points (25, 26) can be calculated as follows: difference between (19,20) to (31)/1.618, hence calculate Meisner's point (25) = difference between (Meisner's point (18) and Meisner's point (31)/1.618 then Meisner's point (26) = difference between Meisner's point (20) to Meisner's point (31)/1.618.

The previous two paragraphs enhance the two algorithms suggested in **Figures 9** and **10** with more than 33 features that can be used in modeling a human face. The features are reflected as a continuum to the first algorithm in **Figure 11**.

Input Total Height of a person (total)
Set M2 = total/2.618
Set M1 = total/1.618
Set M3 = M1/2.618
Set M4 = M1/1.618
Set M5 = M2/1.618
Set M6 = M2/2.618
Set M7 = M3/2.618
Set M8 = M3/1.618
Set M9 = M4/2.618
Set M11 = M4/1.618
Set M12 = M5/1.618
Set M13 = M5/2.618
Set M14 = M6/1.618
Set M15 = M6/2.618
Set M16 = M7/2.618
Set M17 = M7/1.618
Set M18 = M9/2.618
Set M19 = M9/1.618
Set M20 = M11/2.618
Set M21 = M11/1.618
Set M22 = M12/1.618
Set M23 = M12/2.618
Set M24 = M14/1.618
Set M25 = M14/2.618
Set M26 = M15/1.618
Set M27 = M15/2.618
Set M28 = M24/2.618
Set M29 = M24/1.618
The length of the face = M25 + M26 + M29
The width of the face = length of face/1.618
*Left tip of eye brow to the right tip of eye brow = M25 * 1.618*
From tip of eye brow to between the eyes = 2XM25/1.618
Width of shoulders 1/4 of height of a man
The foot is 1/6 of the height of a man

Figure 10. Human body measurements algorithm.

{Horizontal segmentation of human face model}

Meisner's Point (15) =width of face/2.618
Meisner's Point (16) =width of face/2.618
Meisner's Point (13) =width of face/ (2*2.618)
Meisner's Point (14) =width of face/ (2*2.618)
Meisner's Point (7) = Meisner's Point (13)/1.618
Meisner's Point (8) = Meisner's Point (14)/1.618)
Meisner's Point (29) = width of face / (2*1.618)
Meisner's Point (30) = width of face / (2*1.618)
Meisner's Point (24) = half width of face to Meisner's Point (30) / 1.618
Meisner's Point (23) = half width of face to Meisner's Point (30) / 1.618.
Meisner's Points (27,28) are cupid bow hence to derive them divide the distance from Meisner's point (29 to 30)/1.618
Meisner's point (29 to 30) =distance Meisner's point (29 to 30) * 1.618

{Vertical segmentation of the face of human model}

Meisner's point (19) height= length of face/ (1+1.618)
Meisner's point (20) height=face length / (1+1.618)
Meisner's point (21) =face length/1.618
Meisner's point (22) =face length/1.618
Meisner's point (3) = face length/1.618
Meisner's point (4) =face length/1.618
Meisner's point (12) =difference of height between Meisner's point (20) and Meisner's point (4)/1.618 from top
Meisner's point (11) =difference of height between Meisner's point (19) and Meisner's point (3) /1.618 from top
Meisner's point (31) = from Meisner's point (11,12) to Meisner's point (33)/ (1+1.618)
Meisner's point (23) = from Meisner's point (11,12) to Meisner's point (33)/ (1+1.618)
Meisner's point (24) = from Meisner's point (11,12) to Meisner's point (33)/ (1+1.618)
Meisner's point (2) = from Meisner's point (11,12) to Meisner's point (33)/ (1+1.618), measuring from the top
Meisner's point (9) =difference from Meisner's point (3) to Meisner's point (19)/1.618
Meisner's point (10) = difference from Meisner's point (4) to Meisner's point (20)/1.618.
Meisner's point (17) =difference from Meisner's point (9) to Meisner's point (19)/1.618
Meisner's point (18) = difference from Meisner's point (10) to Meisner's point (20)/1.618.
Meisner's point (5) =difference from Meisner's point (3) to Meisner's point (7)/1.618
Meisner's point (6) = difference from Meisner's point (4) to Meisner's point (8)/1.618 from the top.
Meisner's point (32) = the difference between Meisner's point (33) to Meisner's point (31)/1.618 from bottom
Meisner's point (25) = difference between (Meisner's point (18) and Meisner's point (31)/1.618 then Meisner's point (26) = difference between Meisner's point (20) to Meisner's point (31)/1.618.

Figure 11. Human face segmentation a continuum from **Figure 10**.

The hand which is reflected as M20:M21 is 1:1.618, again M5 which is the elbow to tip of the shoulder, M5:M20 is 1:1.618. Hence when modeling a human figure, the following can be derived:

Length of hand name C: length of the arm (B) is proportion to 1:1.618.

Length of arm (B): length of elbow to tip of shoulder (A) is 1:1.618.

The fingers are proportional as follows: from tip of figure to distal phalange (C), from distal phalange to middle phalange is (B), and from middle phalange to proximal phalange is (A). The A:B: C of the whole arm is repeated in the figures proportions. The index finger from tip of the figure to the first knuckles (distal phalange) is proportional to the second knuckle (middle phalange) 1: φ, which is equally similar to middle finger, ring finger, and little finger. The thumb from the tip to the (distal phalange) proportional to the proximal phalange is 1: φ and to the joint connecting the hand is 1: φ 2 as shown in **Figure 10**.

7. Build a human body using golden ratio and suggested algorithm

This section presents two suggested algorithms that calculate all 35 measurements of the human model. The first algorithm shown in **Figure 9** where the input needed is the value of M16. The second algorithm also provides the model with 35 measurements according to golden ratio rules, with the input of the algorithm is the total height of the model. The author experimented with both algorithms and reflected the results in **Tables 2** and **3**. Furthermore, the results are shown on the model in **Figure 12**. The first suggested algorithm is explained next.

To build a human model according to the golden ratio using the rules explained above and suggested in **Figure 6** Bauentwurfslehre by Ernst Neufert, two algorithms are devised in **Figures 9** and **10** that would position the rules as shown next.

First, enter the one basic measurement which is M16 (the length from bottom of feet to ankle). Using the fact implied by formula (1) which is previously explained. Then M17 can be calculated by setting *M17* = M16 × 1.61803398874989. Once *M17* is calculated, then *M7* can be easily determined by using the previously explained formula (2). Furthermore, M8 can be calculated since such fact was established by formula (3).

Hence, M8 = M7 × 1.61803398874989 based on (3). Based on (4), M3 is M3 = M7 + M8. Based on (5), M19 = M18 × 1.61803398874989. Based on (6), M9 = *M18* + *M19*. Based on (7), M21 = M20 × 1.61803398874989. According to (8) M11 = M20 + M21, and according to (9) M4 = M9 + M11, hence and using (10), M4 = M3 × 1.61803398874989. Based on (11) M1 is M1 = M3 + M4, and based on (12) M1 = M2 × 1.61803398874989. According to (13) M2 = M6 + M5, again apply (14) M2 = M5 × 1.61803398874989 and (15) M6 = M2/1.61803398874989. By using (17) and (18) M15 = M6 × 1.61803398874989. Hence, M14 = M6/1.61803398874989; according to (19) M5 = M12 + M13, further according to (20), M12 = M5/1.61803398874989 and based on (21) M13 = M5/2.61803398874989. Based on (22), M12 = M23 + M22 hence M22 = M12/1.61803398874989 and based on (24), M23 = M12/2.61803398874989. Based on (25), M15 = M27 + M26 hence based on (26), M26 = M15/1.61803398874989 and based on (27), M27 = M15/2.61803398874989. According to (28) and the use of (29) and (30), M24 = M14/1.61803398874989 and M25 = M14/2.61803398874989. Again, according to (31) and the use of (32) and (33), M29 = M24/1.61803398874989 and M29 = M24 / 2.61803398874989.

Another version of the algorithm can be suggested when the total height is given, as illustrated in **Figure 10**. The author used a simple Microsoft Excel sheet to calculate the rest by applying the same rules seen in **Table 2**. In order to illustrate the process clearly, an example was set with original value of M16 = 6.13057 cm. To show the results of these simple calculations, the

M1: feet bottom to navel	110.0086
M2: navel to top of head	67.98906
M3: feet bottom to knee bottom line	42.01955
M4: knee bottom line to navel	67.98906
M5: navel to pit of throat and elbow to tip of the shoulder	42.01955
M6: pit of throat to top of head	25.96951
M7: bottom of feet to begin of calves	16.05004
M8: from calves to bottom line of knee	25.96951
M9: bottom line of knee to mid thighs (beginning of finger tips)	25.96951
M11:mid thighs (beginning of finger tips) to navel	42.01955
M12: navel to middle of chest	25.96951
M13: middle of chest to pit of throat	16.05004
M14: pit of throat to point between the eyes	16.05004
M15: point between the eyes to top of head	9.919471
M16: bottom of foot to ankle	6.13057
M17: ankle to beginning of calves	9.919471
M18: beginning of knees to end of knees	9.919471
M19: top of knees to tip of hand fingers	16.05004
M20: hand tip of fingers to hand rest	16.05004
M21: hand rest to elbow and navel to man gentiles	25.96951
M22: navel to beginning of chest (abdomen)	16.05004
M23: beginning of chest to middle of chest	9.919471
M24: throat pit to below nose	9.919471
M25: below nose to top of eyebrows	6.13057
M26: top of eyebrows to hair line	3.788901
M27: hair line to top of head	6.13057
M28: from throat pit to Adam's apple	3.788901
M29: Adam's apple to below the nose	6.13057
The length of the face = M25 + M26 + M29	15.9
The width of the face = length of face/1.618	9.826
Left tip of eyebrow to the right tip of eyebrow = M25 × 1.618	9.869
From tip of eyebrow to between the eyes = 2 × M25/1.618	7.5779
Total height of a man = M1 + M2	177.989
Width of shoulders 1/4 of height of a man	44.49725
The foot is 1/6 of the height of a man	29.666

Table 2. All M's calculated using Microsoft excel sheet.

Enter the height of a man in cm	178
1. The length of the outspread arms is equal to the height of a man	178
2. From the hairline to the bottom of the chin is 1/10 of the height of a man	17.8
3. From below the chin to the top of the head is 1/8 of the height of a man	22.25
4. From above the chest to the top of the head is 1/6 of the height of a man	29.66667
5. From above the chest to the hairline is 1/7 of the height of a man	25.42857
6. The maximum width of the shoulders is ¼ of the height of a man	44.5
7. From the breasts to the top of the head is ¼ of the height of a man	44.5
8. The distance from the elbow to the tip of the hand is ¼ of the height of a man	44.5
9. The distance from the elbow to the armpit is 1/8 of the height of a man	22.25
10. The length of the hand is 1/10 of the height of a man	22.25
11. The root of the penis is at 1/2 the height of a man	89
12. The foot is 1/6 of the height of a man	29.666
13. From below the foot to below the knee is ¼ of the height of a man	44.5
14. From below the knee to the root of the penis is ¼ of the height of a man	44.5
15. The distances from the below the chin to the nose and the eyebrows and the hairline are equal to the ears and to 1/3 of the face	59.33333

Table 3. Proportions and heights as suggested by Vitruvian man model and reflect in **Figure 12.**

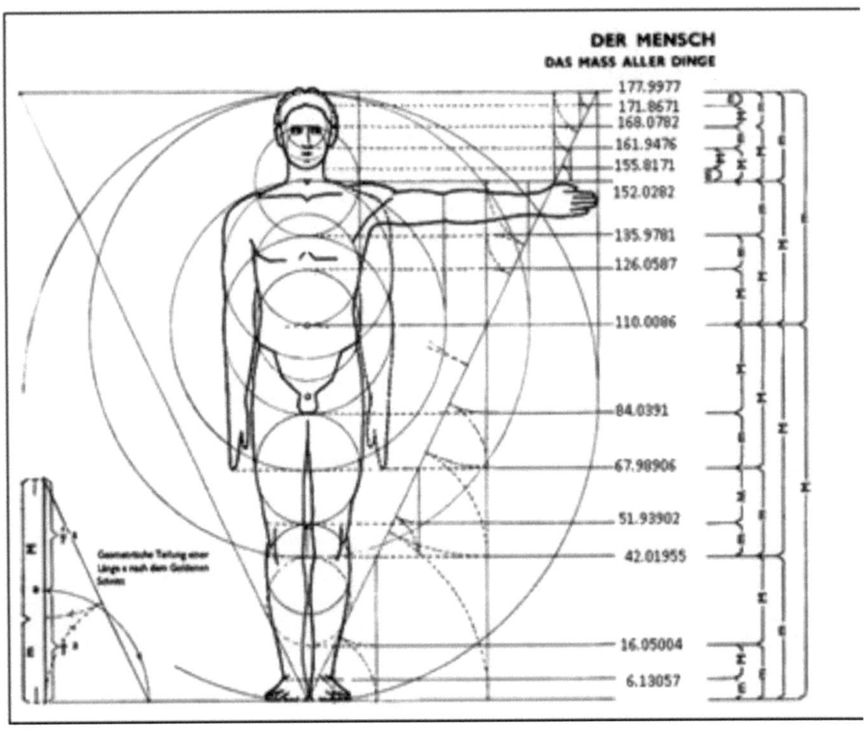

Figure 12. Bauentwurfslehre by Ernst Neufert [14] with heights reflected in centimeters with a base number M16 = 6.1305.

http://dx.doi.org/10.5772/intechopen.76113

numbers were reflected on the same **Figure 10**, while it is worth noting that some interesting facts were realized and seen in **Table 2** as follows: first, M28 and M26 are equal to each other; second, M16, M25, M27, M29 are equal; and third, M15, M17, M18, M23, M24 are equal. Again, M7, M13, M14, M19, M20, M22 are all equal to each other. In addition, M21, M8, M9, M6, M12 are equal to M8 are equal to each other. And M3, M5, and M11 are equal to each other. Finally, M4 and *M2* are equal to each other. Hence, the suggested algorithm can be done with minimum line of code as shown in **Figure 8**:

To build a human body using proportions suggested by Vitruvian Man discussed in the earlier section, then the height intended for the human figure should be designated first (shown in **Figure 12**). As illustrated by **Table 3**, the height entered was 178 cm, whereby using simple calculations, the results are shown in **Table 3**.

8. Conclusion

The goal of this chapter was to enable a multimedia modeler to model a human body using the golden ratio. Hence, the research uncovers 35 measures based on golden ratio introduced by *Bauentwurfslehre* by Ernst Neufert (1936) and Vitruvian Man (The Man in Action) by Leonardo da Vinci. The 67 measurements are: feet bottom to navel, navel to top of head, feet bottom to knee bottom line, knee bottom line to navel, navel to pit of throat & elbow to tip of the shoulder, pit of throat to top of head, bottom of feet to begin of calves, from calves to bottom line of knee, bottom line of knee to mid thighs (beginning of finger tips), mid thighs (beginning of finger tips) to navel, navel to middle of chest, middle of chest to pit of throat, pit of throat to point between the eyes, point between the eyes to top of head, bottom of foot to ankle, ankle to beginning of calves, beginning of knees to end of knees, top of knees to tip of hand fingers (hand toward earth), hand tip of fingers to hand rest, hand rest to elbow and navel to man gentiles, navel to beginning of chest (abdomen), beginning of chest to middle of chest, throat pit to below nose, blow nose to top of eyebrows, top of eyebrows to hair line, hair line to top of head, from throat pit to Adam's apple, Adam's apple to below the nose, the length of the face = M25 + M26 + M29, width of the face = length of face/1.618, left tip of eyebrow to the right tip of eyebrow = M25 × 1.618, from tip of eyebrow to between the eyes = 2 × M25/1.618, width of shoulders 1/4 of height of a man, foot is 1/6 of the height of a man. The measurements are based on 25 proportional rules derived from 15 proportions given by Vitruvian Man and 29 golden proportions in Bauentwurfslehre by Ernst Neufert.

First, the chapter explained the golden section (mathematically, geometrically, arithmetically), then further demonstrated the golden ratio with phi. Furthermore, the chapter discussed Vitruvian Man (The Man in Action) by Leonardo da Vinci. Furthermore, explained *Bauentwurfslehre* by Ernst Neufert. The chapter, then, proposed how to build a human model using the ratios explained and proposed two algorithms that a modeler can follow to build a human body. The algorithms output can be used as proportions and an integral part of design and beauty of nature, to achieve beauty, balance, and harmony, thereby presenting visual parity serving guideline to human body modelers in simulation, gaming, plastic surgery, as well as the world of biometrics or wherever human body measurements and calculations is needed like prosthetic limbs, spatial design, and machine learning of human biometrics. As such, the chapter facilitated and explained for the human modeler, the process of human modeling in multimedia arena. Hence, this research will be a spring board for researchers and practitioners in human modeling in multimedia field.

Author details

Evon Abu-Taieh[1]* and Hamed S. Al-Bdour[2]

*Address all correspondence to: abutaieh@gmail.com

1 Information System Technology, The University of Jordan, Aqaba, Jordan

2 Information System Technology, The University of Jordan, Amman, Jordan

References

[1] Davis TA, Altevogt R. Golden mean of the human body. Fibonacci Quarterly. 1979;**17**:340-384

[2] Dunlap A. The Golden Ratio and Fibonacci Numbers. Singapore: World Scientific Publishing; 1997

[3] Euclid. Elements. 2012. Book 6, Definition 3. http://aleph0.clarku.edu/~djoyce/java/elements/toc.html. Retrieved May 1, 2012

[4] Fett B. An in-depth investigation of the divine ratio. The Montana Mathematics Enthusiast. 2006;**3**(2):157-175

[5] Golden ratio: The divine proportion. (n.d.) Beautiful proportion: http://www.beautiful-proportion.com/2009/08/beautiful-proportions-golden-ratio-also.html. Retrieved May 1, 2012

[6] Lidwell W, Holden K, Butler J. Universal Principles of Design: A Cross-Disciplinary Reference. Gloucester: Rockport Publishers; 2003

[7] Livio M. The Golden Ratio: The Story of Phi, the World's most Astonishing Number. New York: Broadway Books; 2002

[8] Pacioli L. Dedivina proportione, Luca Paganinem de Paganinus de Brescia (Antonio Capella) (1509), Venice. http://en.wikipedia.org/wiki/De_divina_proportione. Retrieved May 1, 2012

[9] Panero J, Zelnik M. Human Dimension & Interior Space: A Source Book of Design Reference Standards. New York: Watson-Guptil Publications; 1979

[10] Sadowski P. The Knight on His Quest: Symbolic Patterns of Transition in Sir Gawain and the Green Knight. Cranbury: Associated University Presses; 1996

[11] Summerson J. Heavenly Mansions: And Other Essays on Architecture. New York: W.W Norton; 1963. p. 37

[12] Taylor P. The Art of Bridging the Gap. From The New Zealand Herald. May 30, 2009. http://www.nzherald.co.nz/auckland-region/news/article.cfm?l_id = 117&objectid = 10575355. Retrieved May 1, 2012

[13] Wolfram. Golden Ratio, Mathworld (n.d.): http://mathworld.wolfram.com/GoldenRatio.html 9/

[14] Word Press Files. Retrieved December 28, 2011. http://thefunambulistdotnet.files.wordpress.com/2012/04/nnj-abb5.gif

[15] Hambidge J. Dynamic Symmetry: The Greek Vase. New Haven: Yale University Press; 1920

[16] Abu-Taieh E. An algorithm for human modeling in information technology multimedia using human biometrics found in golden ratio, vitruvian man and neufert. In: 2015 Fifth International Conference on e-Learning (ECONF); 2015; Manama, pp. 65–73. DOI: 10.1109/ECONF.2015.43.http://ieeexplore.ieee.org/stamp/stamp.jsp?tp=&arnumber=7478214&isnumber=7478193

[17] Abu-Taieh E, El-Maheed M, El-Maheed M, Abu-Tayeh A, Abu-Tayeh J, El-Haj A. Human modeling in information technology multimedia using human biometrics found in golden ratio, Vitruvian man and Neufert. In: Proceedings IBIMA Conference: Innovation Vision 2020, Spain. 2012. pp. 858–869

[18] Golden ratio in art composition and design, Gary Meisner. 2014. https://www.goldennumber.net/art-composition-design/. Retrieved January 25, 2018

[19] Gary Meisner. Meisner beauty guide for golden ratio facial analysis. March 21, 2016. https://www.goldennumber.net/meisner-beauty-guide-golden-ratio-facial-analysis/

[20] Neufert E. Architects' Data. Blackwell Science. 1936. http://www.vgloop.com/_files/1403617229-311131.pdf

[21] Markowsky, George. Misconceptions about the golden ratio. College Mathematics Journal. January 1992;**23**(1):2-19